T0289380

Skills for a Modern Ukraine

DIRECTIONS IN DEVELOPMENT
Human Development

Skills for a Modern Ukraine

Ximena Del Carpio, Olga Kupets, Noël Muller, and Anna Olefir

 WORLD BANK GROUP

© 2017 International Bank for Reconstruction and Development / The World Bank
1818 H Street NW, Washington, DC 20433
Telephone: 202-473-1000; Internet: www.worldbank.org

Some rights reserved

1 2 3 4 19 18 17 16

This work is a product of the staff of The World Bank with external contributions. The findings, interpretations, and conclusions expressed in this work do not necessarily reflect the views of The World Bank, its Board of Executive Directors, or the governments they represent. The World Bank does not guarantee the accuracy of the data included in this work. The boundaries, colors, denominations, and other information shown on any map in this work do not imply any judgment on the part of The World Bank concerning the legal status of any territory or the endorsement or acceptance of such boundaries.

Nothing herein shall constitute or be considered to be a limitation upon or waiver of the privileges and immunities of The World Bank, all of which are specifically reserved.

Rights and Permissions

This work is available under the Creative Commons Attribution 3.0 IGO license (CC BY 3.0 IGO) http://creativecommons.org/licenses/by/3.0/igo. Under the Creative Commons Attribution license, you are free to copy, distribute, transmit, and adapt this work, including for commercial purposes, under the following conditions:

Attribution—Please cite the work as follows: Del Carpio, Ximena, Olga Kupets, Noël Muller, and Anna Olefir. 2017. *Skills for a Modern Ukraine*. Directions in Development. Washington, DC: World Bank. doi:10.1596/978-1-4648-0890-6. License: Creative Commons Attribution CC BY 3.0 IGO

Translations—If you create a translation of this work, please add the following disclaimer along with the attribution: *This translation was not created by The World Bank and should not be considered an official World Bank translation. The World Bank shall not be liable for any content or error in this translation.*

Adaptations—If you create an adaptation of this work, please add the following disclaimer along with the attribution: *This is an adaptation of an original work by The World Bank. Views and opinions expressed in the adaptation are the sole responsibility of the author or authors of the adaptation and are not endorsed by The World Bank.*

Third-party content—The World Bank does not necessarily own each component of the content contained within the work. The World Bank therefore does not warrant that the use of any third-party-owned individual component or part contained in the work will not infringe on the rights of those third parties. The risk of claims resulting from such infringement rests solely with you. If you wish to re-use a component of the work, it is your responsibility to determine whether permission is needed for that re-use and to obtain permission from the copyright owner. Examples of components can include, but are not limited to, tables, figures, or images.

All queries on rights and licenses should be addressed to World Bank Publications, The World Bank Group, 1818 H Street NW, Washington, DC 20433, USA; fax: 202-522-2625; e-mail: pubrights@worldbank.org.

ISBN (paper): 978-1-4648-0890-6
ISBN (electronic): 978-1-4648-0891-3
DOI: 10.1596/978-1-4648-0890-6

Cover photo: Aec and Waone (Interesni Kazki). Used with permission; further permission required for reuse.
Cover design: Debra Naylor, Naylor Design, Inc.

Library of Congress Cataloging-in-Publication Data has been requested.

Contents

Boxes

Figures

Maps

Tables

Acknowledgments

This report was prepared by Ximena Del Carpio, Olga Kupets, Noël Muller, and Anna Olefir. Numerous World Bank colleagues supported the authors. Johannes Koettl and Indhira Santos initiated the task and led the extensive data collection efforts. Maria Laura Sanchez Puerta and Alexandria Valerio led the data collection protocol of the Skills toward Employment and Productivity (STEP) surveys. Hernan Winkler wrote a box on the supply and demand for information technology workers. Paolo Belli, Qimiao Fan, and Andrew Mason provided general guidance. Peer reviewers Wendy Cunningham, Halil Dundar, Dhushshyanth Raju, and Hernan Winkler provided excellent comments and advice.

Paolo Belli, Igor Kheyfets, Klavdiya Maksymenko, Katherine Patrick, Abla Safir, and Yulia Smolyar provided valuable inputs, intellectual support, and practical advice throughout the development of this study. The authors also gratefully acknowledge the excellent administrative support of Anna Goodman, Oleksandra 'Sasha' Griaznova, and Anastasia Soltis, and editing support of Sarah Ying Zou.

The team is grateful to the government of Ukraine and representatives of the private sector for sharing their impressions and views on findings at an early stage of the study. In particular, it would like to thank the Ministry of Social Policy, the State Employment Service, the Ministry of Education and Science, and the Confederation of Employers of Ukraine.

The collection of the household and employer skills surveys benefited from the support and cooperation of partners at the Eurasia Competitiveness Programme of the Organisation for Economic Co-operation and Development (OECD), the Institute for the Study of Labor (IZA), the Kyiv International Institute of Sociology (KIIS), and Tetyana Sytnyk and her colleagues from Gesellschaft für Konsumforschung (GfK).

About the Authors

Ximena Del Carpio, a Peruvian and U.S. national, is a program leader in the World Bank's Social Protection and Labor Global Practice, where she leads research and operations and works with client countries to develop and implement policies to improve social protection and access to labor markets and economic opportunities. Her analytical and operational work focuses on social policy, migration, skills in the labor market, and labor regulations, especially in East Asia and Pacific, Eastern Europe and Central Asia, and Latin America. Prior to that, she worked in the World Bank's Independent Evaluation Group, where she led a range of impact evaluations of economic development programs in Latin American and African countries. Before joining the Bank, she worked at the RAND Corporation and at the Minority Business Development Agency of the U.S. Department of Commerce. She holds a PhD in political economics from the University of Southern California and a dual masters in business administration and public policy from Pepperdine University in the United States.

Olga Kupets, a Ukrainian national, is a professor at the Kyiv School of Economics in Ukraine and a consultant to the World Bank. She conducts empirical research on education, employment and the labor market, social policies, and development of transition countries in Ukraine and the Eastern Europe and Central Asia region. She has worked as associate professor of economics at the National University of Kyiv-Mohyla Academy and as a local consultant to the International Labour Organization (ILO), the United States Agency for International Development (USAID), and the European Training Foundation (ETF). She holds a PhD in economics from the Institute of Demography and Social Studies of the Ukrainian National Academy of Sciences and a master's degree in economics from the Kyiv School of Economics and in mathematics and computer science from Cherkasy National University in Ukraine.

Noël Muller, a French national, is a consultant economist in the World Bank's Social Protection and Labor Global Practice, where he conducts empirical research and supports Bank teams in Latin America and Ukraine in advising countries on the development of social and employment programs. His research focuses on skills development, the role of skills in the labor market, employment policies, and the constraints faced by jobless and vulnerable workers.

Before joining the Bank, he worked at the Organisation for Economic Co-operation and Development (OECD) Development Centre in France. He holds a master's degree in international and development economics from the University Paris-Dauphine and a bachelor's degree in economics from the University Paris I Pantheon-Sorbonne in France.

Anna Olefir, a Ukrainian national, is an education specialist in the World Bank's Education Global Practice, where she works on education, skills, and the labor market in a number of countries including Belarus, Ethiopia, Kazakhstan, Moldova, Uganda, and Ukraine. Before joining the Bank, she worked for the Canadian International Development Agency in Ukraine as the coordinator of the Canada Fund, which supports the enhancement of economic and social life of people through grassroots democratic governance initiatives. She also served as a lead economist at Ukraine's Ministry of Economy. She holds a PhD in international economics from the Kyiv National Economic University in Ukraine and an MRes in educational and social research from the University of London in the United Kingdom.

Executive Summary

Ukraine's economic progress has been uneven since the start of the transition in 1991. Productivity is low partly because of the slow pace of market-oriented reforms and the misallocation of the labor force. Half of all workers work in low-productivity sectors, one worker out of five is informal, underemployment is widespread, and the rate of inactivity among older people is among the highest in Europe. Demographic factors—including low mobility, rapid aging, and the decline in the population—are also constraining growth. The recent conflict and economic downturn add urgency to the situation.

One the key factors limiting productivity gains is the inadequacy of workforce skills, the focus of this report. The level of skills does not necessarily equate with educational attainment: A diploma does not guarantee that graduates perform well in the workplace. Looking directly at prospective employees' skills—formed in and out of school—provides a more accurate view of human capital than years of schooling.

Indeed, a large body of recent empirical work documents the importance of skills, rather than formal educational attainment, in fostering employment and raising productivity. Developing skills increases employability and enables workers to carry out their jobs more efficiently, use new technology, and innovate. Hiring people with better skills allows firms to move up the value chain.

This study aims to provide policy makers in Ukraine with new evidence to influence the design and implementation of public policies on postsecondary education, labor market information and intermediation, and labor policies. To do so, it investigates the nature of skills valued in Ukraine's labor market, identifies labor shortages, assesses constraints to firms' operations, discusses how institutions affect investment in skills, and suggests policy options. The report provides granular evidence from original data from household and firm skills surveys, a data set of online job vacancies, and an assessment of workforce development institutions.

Five key messages emerge from the analysis:

1. Across occupations and sectors, workers need a mix of advanced cognitive, socioemotional, and technical skills to be successful in the labor market.
2. Postsecondary education and training lack relevance for today's labor market.

3. Institutional factors are hindering the efficient allocation of labor and skills development.
4. Gaps in skills are limiting productivity.
5. A range of policies could enhance the development and use of skills.

Message 1: Workers Need a Mix of Skills

Skills are the abilities to perform tasks and respond to situations. They include competencies, attitudes, beliefs, and behaviors that are modifiable across the life cycle and can be learned and improved through specific programs and policies.

Skills can be divided into in three broad overlapping sets:

- **Cognitive skills** can be defined as intelligence or mental abilities. They include basic academic knowledge (such as literacy) and more complex thinking (such as critical thinking and problem-solving).
- **Socioemotional skills** are behaviors, attitudes, and personality traits (such as the ability to manage emotions, achieve goals, and work with others) that enable individuals to navigate personal and social situations effectively.
- **Technical skills** are the specific knowledge needed to perform a task as well as physical skills.

The analysis shows that workers need a mix of advanced cognitive, socioemotional, and technical skills to succeed in the labor market—a finding that is in line with evidence from around the world. A set of skills are highly valued across sectors and types of occupations (table ES.1).

Message 2: Postsecondary Education and Training Lack Relevance for Today's Labor Market

Ukrainians have high levels of basic cognitive skills, but the higher education and training system does not produce enough skills relevant for today's labor market. Ukrainian firms in key sectors report that the lack of adequate skills is one of the

Table ES.1 Core Cognitive, Socioemotional, and Technical Skills Identified as Most Valued in Ukraine

Type of skill	Specific skills
Cognitive	Problem solving, communication, creative and critical thinking, time management, learning, foreign language
Socioemotional	Resilience (stress resistance and perseverance), ethics, achievement motivation (goal orientation and motivation to learn), teamwork
Technical	Sales skills, knowledge of markets and products, analytical methods, proficiency in field-specific software, knowledge of legislations, web programming, design, basic computer tools, driving

Sources: ULMS-STEP Household Survey 2012; Ukraine STEP Employer Surveys 2014; and job vacancies from HeadHunter online job portal 2015.

most important constraints to hiring. Most employers surveyed believe that the education system does not produce enough people with practical skills, the right kind or level of skills, or up-to-date knowledge.

Message 3: Institutional Factors Are Hindering the Efficient Allocation of Labor and Skills Development

Five institutional factors are hindering skills development and the efficient allocation of labor:

1. The formal education and training system is not providing students with the skills employers need, and it suffers from weak governance and an inefficient funding system.
2. Skills training outside the formal education system has very low take-up rates. Partnerships between firms and education institutions are scarce, with only a fifth of firms in key sectors maintaining regular contacts with educational and training institutions.
3. Employers see payroll taxes and social security contributions as major constraints to their operation and growth. (Other major constraints include economic and financial uncertainty, political instability, corruption, and crime.)
4. Little reliable information is available on current and emerging skills demands that would allow students, educators, and training providers to make good decisions or make their program offerings relevant to labor market conditions.
5. Despite recent changes, the labor code and other labor market institutions do not facilitate an adaptable labor market or foster conditions that are conducive for the creation of more and better jobs.

Message 4: Skills Gaps Are Limiting Productivity

Skills gaps significantly constrain firms' performance in Ukraine: 40 percent of firms in four key sectors (agriculture, food processing, information technology, and renewable energy) report a significant gap between the type of skills their employees have and those they need to achieve their business objectives. Although skills gaps are not the most pressing constraint firms face, they limit companies' ability to hire, perform, and grow.

Message 5: A Range of Policies Could Enhance the Development and Use of Skills

Policy options can be organized into three pillars (table ES.2):

- Building foundational skills for new labor market entrants
- Enhancing the development of advanced skills for current and future workers
- Improving the institutional environment to facilitate the use of skills

Table ES.2 Overview of Policy Proposals for Improving Skills in Ukraine

Policy pillar	Components
Build foundational skills	Integrate socioemotional development into traditional learning
	Develop a lifelong skills development strategy
Enhance the development of advanced skills	Build and upgrade qualification and occupational standards
	Introduce financial incentives for firms to promote training
	Enhance the labor market information system
	Build stronger tertiary education leadership structure
	Introduce results-based funding of postsecondary education and training institutions
Improve the institutional environment	Reform the labor code (labor costs, contracts, worker protection)
	Build a statistical profiling tool for employment services
	Remove barriers to internal migration

Pillar 1: Building foundational skills for new labor market entrants

Skills formation is a cumulative process. Interventions have to be implemented as an integrated set across the life cycle, introduced when individuals are biologically and socially ready to acquire particular skills. The benefits of an investment depend on an individual's existing level of skills.

The home learning environment plays an important role in shaping the formation of cognitive and socioemotional skills. Technical skills are developed after childhood, through informal learning, formal schooling, training, and on-the-job learning. Individuals need to acquire good foundational skills if they are to be able to learn, thrive at school and in the labor market, gain more advanced skills, and adapt to rapidly changing labor market needs.

A variety of interventions can foster socioemotional skills. Interventions are characterized by specific objectives, targeting age period—preschool, school age, youth, and adult age—and places of implementation such as school, work, or centers. Interventions for socioemotional learning must target optimal periods for the development of key skills.

Pillar 2: Enhancing the development of advanced skills for current and future workers

Building a strong postsecondary education leadership structure and adopting performance-based financing are promising ways to improve the relevance and quality of postsecondary education. Links between education institutions and private sector firms need to be created. The private sector needs to participate in setting up occupation standards and adapting curricula to the needs of the marketplace.

On-the-job training is an effective way for workers to build advanced skills. The government could provide financial incentives to firms to offer such training, linking them to performance criteria and fund-matching mechanisms to prevent abuse.

Pillar 3: Improving the institutional environment to facilitate the use of skills

Job creation can be encouraged through labor regulation reforms (while ensuring that workers benefit from sufficient social protection). Labor costs can be reduced and contractual diversity increased by shifting toward a flexicurity-like model (with income or activity support instead of rigid job protection). Job creation can also be spurred by encouraging entrepreneurship, through training, access to finance, and advisory services and networking.

A better information system on the labor market is essential to facilitate investments in skills formation and identify demand for skills. Students, their families, and job seekers should have access to reliable information on labor market prospects, job requirements, and wages across fields. The State Employment Service could collect and continuously update information on job vacancies and job requirements (using a methodology similar to the one used in this report).

Removing barriers to internal migration would make it easier for workers to find job opportunities and make full use of their skills. Internal migration could be facilitated by ensuring the portability of social benefits and removing administrative procedures that require people to be officially registered at their place of residence.

Abbreviations

ALMP	active labor market program
CAP	Certified Accounting Practitioner
CCC	City College of Chicago
CFA	Chartered Financial Analyst
CIDA	Canadian International Development Agency
CIMA	Chartered Institute of Management Accountants
CIPA	Certified International Professional Accountant
CVET	continuing vocational education and training
DipIFR	Diploma in International Financial Reporting
ETF	European Training Foundation
ETS	Educational Testing Services
GDP	gross domestic product
GfK	Gesellschaft für Konsumforschung
ICT	information and communication technologies
IDP	internally displaced people
ILO	International Labour Organization
ISCED	International Standard Classification of Education
ISCO	International Standard Classification of Occupations
IT	information technology
IVET	initial vocational education and training
IZA	Institute for the Study of Labor
KIIS	Kyiv International Institute of Sociology
LMIS	labor market information system
NGO	nongovernmental organization
NQF	National Qualification Framework
OECD	Organisation for Economic Co-operation and Development
PC	personal computer
PIAAC	Programme for the International Assessment of Adults' Competencies

PRACTICE	taxonomy of socioemotional skills: (social) problem solving, resilience, achievement motivation, control, teamwork, initiative, confidence, and ethics
SABER	Systems Approach for Better Education Results
SES	State Employment Service
STEP	Skills toward Employment and Productivity
SWIFT	Society for Worldwide Interbank Financial Telecommunication
TIMSS	Trends in International Mathematics and Science Study
TVET/VET	technical vocational education and training/vocational education and training
ULMS	Ukrainian Longitudinal Monitoring Survey
USAID	United States Agency for International Development
USC	unified social contribution
WfD	workforce development (system)

Overview

Providing workers with the skills they need to secure good jobs and perform them well is a critical policy challenge in Ukraine, where many employers decry skills deficits and mismatches. Drawing on several sources of original data, this report provides evidence on the importance of three types of skills (advanced cognitive, socioemotional, and technical skills); identifies the skills employers seek; and proposes ways in which policy makers can reform the country's training institutions and labor laws to increase employment, raise productivity, and put Ukraine on a higher-growth pathway.

Stagnation following Independence

Under Soviet rule, Ukraine was home to abundant natural resources, a range of industries, and a workforce with high educational attainment. Independence seemed to promise broad-based prosperity. In the early 1990s, its per capita gross domestic product was similar to that of other middle-income countries (such as Brazil, Poland, and Turkey).

Today, Ukraine still has relatively high literacy rates, large numbers of university students, and significant numbers of graduates who contribute to industrial and scientific progress (World Bank 2011). But economic performance has been tenuous at best, productivity is lower than in comparable countries, and the standard of living for the average person was lower in 2015 than it was 25 years ago.

One of the main causes of this disappointing economic performance is the lack or slow pace of reform, especially of policies that regulate labor markets and education and training institutions. The labor code was drafted in 1971 and amended only marginally over the years; it therefore still includes many pretransition features. The antiquated code limits incentives for firms to hire and grow and leads to informal employment, underemployment, and wage arrears.

Stagnation in vocational and postsecondary instruction hinders the ability of training and education institutions to respond to the rapidly changing needs of the labor market. Underfinancing and limited technical capacity have constrained the implementation of reforms that have been approved—and the effectiveness of the reforms that have been implemented is unclear. Population decline and the low internal mobility of the labor force also hold back growth.

As a result of these factors, Ukraine ranks in the bottom tier of countries on indicators rating the ease of doing business. In 2014 it placed 96th out of 189 countries, below most other countries in Eastern Europe and Central Asia (World Bank 2014).

The conflict in eastern Ukraine and an economic downturn further weaken labor market prospects and economic performance more broadly. Since the beginning of the conflict in February 2014, employment has declined, as a result of the loss of job opportunities in Crimea and the near cessation of economic activities in the Donbas region, an important mining extraction and manufacturing area of the country. As of early 2015, 800,000 jobs had been lost in the Donbas region alone. In 2014–15 more than a million people migrated to another part of Ukraine or neighboring countries. Significant employment adjustment has also taken place through reduced hours, unpaid administrative leaves, and wage arrears, which more than tripled between 2014 and 2015, from Hrv 753 million to Hrv 2,437 million.

The Importance of Skills in Boosting Employment and Productivity

A large body of empirical work documents the importance of skills, rather than just formal educational achievement, in fostering employment and productivity (see reviews by Borghans and others 2008, Almlund and others 2011, Kautz and others 2014, and OECD 2015). Skills increase employability; enable workers to perform their jobs more efficiently, use new technology, and innovate; and allow firms to move up value chains (Banerji and others 2010; Arias and others 2014). A better skills development strategy has the potential to overcome structural challenges by improving firms' performance and increasing the productivity of the Ukrainian economy.

The term *skills* refers to competencies, attitudes, beliefs, and behaviors that are malleable across an individual's development and can be learned. Schools are a privileged place for teaching skills, but they are not the only venue where skills are formed. Family background, the living environment, extracurricular activities, and the workplace all affect skills development.

Skills are multidimensional and can be categorized into three broad overlapping sets (figure O.1):

- **Cognitive skills** can be defined as intelligence or mental abilities. They include basic academic knowledge (such as literacy) and more complex thinking (such as critical thinking and problem-solving).

Figure O.1 Framework for Cognitive, Socioemotional, and Technical Skills

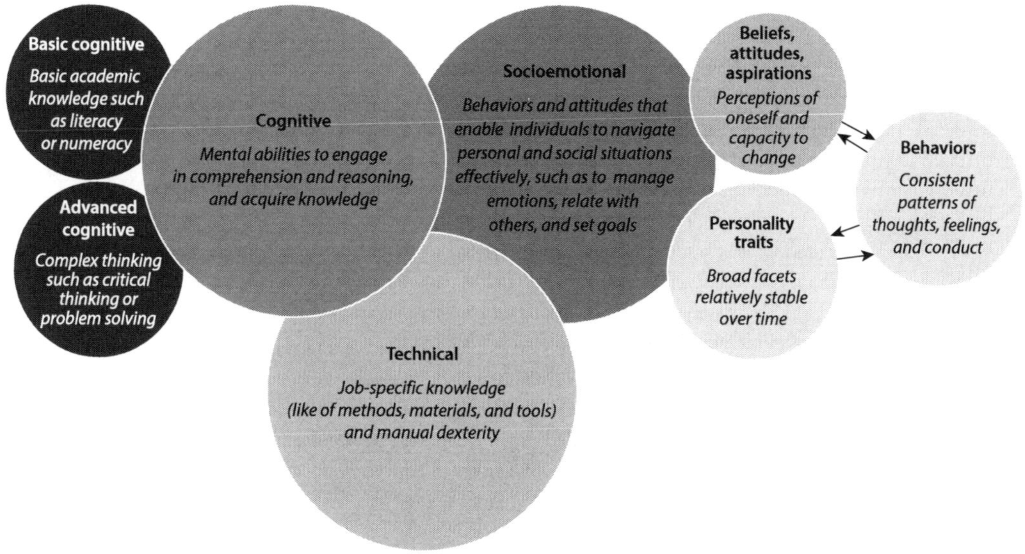

Sources: Borghans and others 2008; Roberts 2009; Almlund and others 2011; OECD 2015.

- **Socioemotional skills** are behaviors, attitudes, and personality traits that enable individuals to navigate personal and social situations effectively (by managing emotions, achieving goals, and working well with others, for example).
- **Technical skills** can be defined as the specific knowledge needed to carry out one's job as well as physical dexterity.

Employer Demand for Advanced Cognitive, Socioemotional, and Technical Skills

Skills gaps are significantly constraining firms' performance in Ukraine. In a 2014 survey of four key sectors (agriculture, food processing, information technology [IT], and renewable energy), 40 percent of firms reported significant gaps between the skills their employees have and the skills they need to achieve the firm's business objectives (figure O.2). About half of all firms in food processing and IT (a sector in which most employees have postsecondary education levels) decry the lack of skills. The lack of skills is less salient in the agriculture and renewable energy sectors, but at least 20 percent of firms in both of those sectors report that skills are inadequate.

Skills gaps limit a company's efficiency, service quality, and ability to retain and grow its client base. They make it difficult for firms to hire the right people, especially in higher-skilled occupations and in occupational categories that require job-specific technical skills.

What are the skills that employers value and lament the lack of? The most highly demanded skills are a mix of advanced cognitive, socioemotional,

Figure O.2 Problems Related to Skills Gaps Cited by Ukrainian Firms in Four Key Sectors

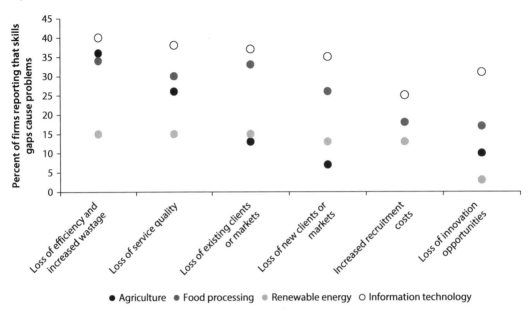

● Agriculture   ● Food processing   ● Renewable energy   ○ Information technology

Source: Ukraine STEP Employer Survey 2014.
Note: Skills gap refers to the gap between the skills a firm's employees have and the skills the firm needs to achieve its business objectives.

Table O.1 Skills Requirements Frequently Cited in Job Vacancies in Ukraine, March 2015

Type of skill	Specific requirements
Advanced cognitive	Communication, learning, time management, analytical skills, foreign languages, multitasking, critical thinking, problem solving, decision making
Socioemotional	Responsibility, stress resistance, self-management, goal orientation, teamwork, negotiation, organization, professionalism, teamwork, cooperation (agreeableness), accuracy (attention to detail), leadership, and perseverance
Technical	Sales skills, knowledge of markets and products, analytical methods, proficiency in field-specific software, knowledge of legislations, web programming, design, basic computer tools

Source: Job vacancies on HeadHunter online portal, March 2015.
Note: The HeadHunter portal targets high-skilled occupations. Skills requirements are therefore likely to be more representative of these types of occupations than of all occupations.

and technical skills. The results of the 2014 Ukraine STEP (Skills Toward Employment and Productivity) Employer Survey and a data set of 2015 job vacancies show that advanced cognitive skills that allow workers to analyze and solve problems, manage their time, gain new knowledge and learn new methods, and communicate effectively are highly demanded in Ukraine (table O.1). Employers look for workers who not only think well but who also possess socioemotional skills, including the ability to manage their emotions and behaviors (self-management, resilience, ethics); set goals and be willing to learn (achievement motivation); and work well with others (teamwork). A core set of technical skills is harder to define, because they are often occupation- or job-specific, and the only source of detailed technical skills (the job vacancy data set created for this report) tends to target higher-skilled occupations. With this caveat in mind, a range of employers looks for sales skills, knowledge of markets and products, and computer skills.

The skills employers value most are consistent across sectors and occupations. Employers from the four key sectors surveyed ranked the top five (out of 14) skills virtually identically (table O.2):

1. job-specific technical skills (technical)
2. professional behavior (socioemotional)
3. problem solving (advanced cognitive)
4. ability to work independently (socioemotional)
5. teamwork (socioemotional)

These skills are equally important for high-skilled and low- and middle-skilled occupations. This uniformity is remarkable given the diversity of these sectors with regard to location, size, number of jobs, occupational structure, and extent of reported skills gaps.

Skills and Labor Market Outcomes of Urban Ukrainians

Ukrainians in urban areas have good basic cognitive skills (the ability to evaluate and reflect from written text). These skills levels are roughly equivalent to levels in Organisation for Economic Co-operation and Development (OECD) countries; they are higher than in all middle-income countries for which comparable data are available.

Skills are relatively well distributed across demographic groups, but large gaps exist across generations. Adults educated during the transition years (people who were 34–45 in 2014) have significantly lower average levels of basic cognitive skills than their older or younger peers (figure O.3).

Differences in socioemotional skills across age, gender, or educational level are modest. These skills cannot be meaningfully compared across countries, because they tend to be driven by culture.

Ukrainian workers with strong skills—particularly strong socioemotional skills—have better labor market outcomes than people with weaker skills. People in Ukraine who are creative, proactive, perseverant, responsible, adaptable, and emotionally stable earn more, have higher occupational status, and are more likely to be active in the labor market. Basic cognitive skills do not appear to be significantly associated with these outcomes (possibly because employers simply assume that prospective workers have these skills).

The importance of cognitive and socioemotional skills, as well as other factors, varies across age groups and occupation type. Skills, especially socioemotional skills, explain more of the wage difference among youth (15–29) and older workers (45–64) than among middle-age workers (30–44) (figure O.4). Among older workers, socioemotional skills, in particular grit (perseverance) and openness to

Table O.2 Skills and Labor Needs of Ukrainian Firms and Skills Gaps in Key Sectors

Sector	Main regions	Five most valued skills	Percent of firms reporting significant skills gap in their workforce	Three most demanded occupational categories	Top three occupational groups with major skills gaps	Top five occupations with major skills gaps
Agribusiness growers	Dnipropetrovsk, Odessa, Mykolaiv	1. Job-specific technical 2. Professional behavior 3. Problem solving 4. Ability to work independently 5. Teamwork	48	1. Laborer 2. Machine operator 3. Technician	1. Machine operator 2. Craftsperson 3. Skilled agricultural worker	1. Laborer 2. Tractor driver 3. Dairy and livestock producers 4. Repair worker 5. Veterinarian
Agribusiness food processors	Kyiv City, Kyiv Oblast, Dnipropetrovsk, Kharkiv	1. Job-specific technical 2. Professional behavior 3. Problem solving 4. Teamwork 5. Ability to work independently	45	1. Laborer 2. Technician 3. Machine operator	1. Craftsperson 2. Technician 3. Machine operator	1. Laborer 2. Service and shop worker 3. Associate professional in food technology 4. Baker and pastry chef 5. Shop assistant
Renewable energy	Kyiv City, Lviv, Cherkasy	1. Job-specific technical 2. Problem solving	29	1. Professional 2. Craftsperson	1. Professional 2. Technician	1. Machine operator 2. Cartographer and surveyor

table continues next page

Table O.2 Skills and Labor Needs of Ukrainian Firms and Skills Gaps in Key Sectors *(continued)*

Sector	Main regions	Five most valued skills	Percent of firms reporting significant skills gap in their workforce	Three most demanded occupational categories	Top three occupational groups with major skills gaps	Top five occupations with major skills gaps
		3. Creative and critical thinking		3. Laborer	3. Clerk	3. Civil engineer
		4. Professional behavior				4. Geologist and geophysicist
		5. Teamwork				5. Technology guide bioenergy installer
Information and communication technology	Kyiv City, Kharkiv, Dnipropetrovsk	1. Job-specific technical	21	1. Professional	1. Technician	1. Computer assistant
		2. Problem solving		2. Technician	2. Professional	2. Programmer
		3. Professional behavior		3. Clerk	3. Clerk	3. Service and shop worker
		4. Ability to work independently				4. Computer system designer and analyst
		5. Teamwork				5. Diverse types of clerks

Source: Ukraine STEP Employer Survey 2014.

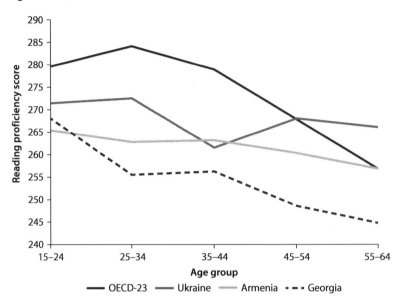

Figure O.3 Average Adult Reading Proficiency Levels in Selected Countries, by Age Cohort, 2012

Sources: Armenia, Colombia, Georgia, and Vietnam: STEP Household Surveys 2012–13. Ukraine: ULMS-STEP Household Survey 2012. OECD: Programme for the International Assessment of Adults' Competencies (PIAAC) 2012–13.
Note: Data for Armenia, Georgia, and Ukraine are for urban areas only. Data for 23 OECD countries (OECD-23) are national. Reading proficiency scores range from 0 (lowest) to 500 (highest). For a description of reading scores, see table A.2 in appendix A.

experience (enjoyment of learning and being receptive to new ideas), are associated with the largest wage variation.

Observable factors other than skills—including demographics, job function, and location—explain a larger portion of wage variations. Potential work experience (the difference between the person's age and the approximate age at the end of his or her studies) matters greatly for youth, and gender is important for middle-age adults, reflecting the disproportionate representation of women in low-paid sectors (education, health care, retail trade, individual services).

Reforming Education and Training to Meet the Needs of the Workplace
The workforce development system, including education and training institutions, needs to be reformed to respond to today's labor market needs. This includes focusing on the development of skills that are in demand rather than achieving a given level of education (in particular at the postsecondary level), completing traditional cognitive and technical learning with socioemotional learning, and improving education and training institution governance.

Including Socioemotional Skills in Conventional Learning
Formal education and training programs rarely teach socioemotional skills, even though people with higher levels of such skills are more successful

Figure O.4 Factors Associated with Variation in Hourly Wages in Urban Ukraine, by Age Group and Occupation, 2012

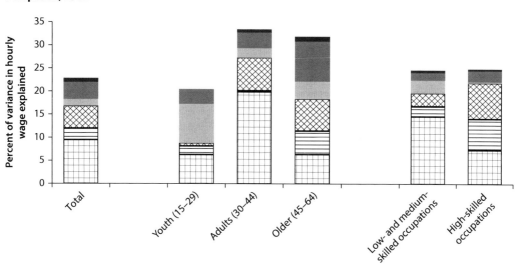

Source: ULMS-STEP Household Survey 2012.
Note: Results obtained using a Fields regression-based decomposition of the log of hourly wages (Fields 2003). The height of each bar represents the total variation in wages explained by the data used for that regression (coefficient of determination = R^2). The subcomponents of each bar show the contribution of each factor to total wage variation. Cognitive skills refer to reading proficiency. Socioemotional skills include openness to experience, conscientiousness, extroversion, agreeableness, emotional stability, grit, hostile attribution bias, and decision making. Potential work experience is the difference between the person's age and the approximate age at the end of his or her studies (it also includes a squared term). Family background refers to mother's education and main language spoken at home (Ukrainian, Russian, both, or neither).

in school and at work and have better health and other social outcomes (Heckman, Stixrud, and Urzúa 2006; Borghans and others 2008, Almlund and others 2011; Kautz and others 2014; and OECD 2015). Socioemotional skills are not a substitute for cognitive or technical skills but act as a pedestal to learn better, strive, and achieve labor market success. Socioemotional skills are by nature malleable and therefore can be fostered through interventions. These skills are highly demanded by employers and should be part of a comprehensive skills development strategy.

A core set of socioemotional skills emerges from the analysis of job vacancies and household and firm surveys conducted for this report (table O.3). It includes skills that help people manage their emotions and behaviors (control, resilience, ethics); set goals and be willing to learn (achievement motivation); and work with others (teamwork). These skills are best acquired and reinforced at particular points in the life cycle.

Rethinking Postsecondary Education and Training Institutions

Ukraine's education system lacks flexibility, quality standards, and relevance for today's labor market needs. Sixty percent of firms in the four key sectors

Table O.3 Socioemotional Skills Demanded by Employers in Ukraine, according to Various Taxonomies

Skills demanded by Ukrainian firms	Equivalent in PRACTICE taxonomy of labor-market oriented skills	Associated Big Five personality traits
Professional behavior	Control and ethics	Conscientiousness
Self-management	Control	Conscientiousness
Stress resistance and perseverance	Resilience	Conscientiousness (grit), emotional stability
Goal orientation and motivation to learn	Achievement motivation	Conscientiousness (grit), openness to experience
Teamwork	Teamwork	Extroversion, agreeableness
Leadership	Initiative	Conscientiousness, openness to experience

Sources: Guerra, Modecki, and Cunningham 2014; Ukraine STEP Employer Survey 2014; HeadHunter job vacancy data set 2015.
Note: PRACTICE (an acronym for Problem Solving, Resilience, Achievement Motivation, Control, Teamwork, Initiative, Confidence, and Ethics) is a taxonomy of labor-market oriented skills elaborated by Guerra, Modecki, and Cunningham (2014).

report that formal education institutions do not provide students with the skills employers need (figure O.5). They claim that the system produces too few people with practical skills, the right kind or level of skills, up-to-date knowledge, good attitude, and self-discipline.

Most adults in Ukraine complete at least upper-secondary school, and almost half have tertiary diplomas. Ukraine also performs well on international student assessments such as Trends in International Mathematics and Science Study (TIMSS), ranking in the same group as high-income countries like Italy, Norway, and Sweden. There are questions, however, about the relevance of education received before the transition (often vocational) and when students should be tracked into technical vocational education and training (TVET) schools. As a result, employers have difficulties to discern skill levels solely based on the education level of the person.

The government has crafted strategies to boost school quality and relevance, but the lack of financial resources and the ad hoc coordination of stakeholders has prevented it from implementing many of them. Funding for vocational training is not based on explicit criteria with performance indicators, and coordination between various government agencies and nongovernment actors is weak.

Many formal postsecondary education and training institutions need to be reformed to improve their strategic framework, system oversight, and service delivery. Ukraine's workforce development system is weak by international standards (figure O.6).[1] Education and training institutions lack clear direction for policy elaboration and implementation; the fragmentation of responsibilities makes it difficult to agree on a common vision, devise policy, and coordinate with employers. The funding system inefficiently allocates resources, adversely affecting the provision of textbooks and the ability to upgrade obsolete infrastructure and equipment of vocational schools.

Figure O.5 Ukrainian Firms' Views of Preparation of Students for the Workplace in Four Sectors

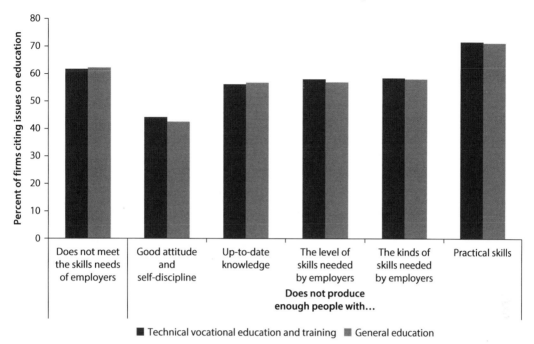

Source: Ukraine STEP Employer Survey 2014.
Note: Data are for firms in four sectors: agriculture, food processing, information technology, and renewable energy.

Figure O.6 Assessment of Ukraine's Workforce Development System

Source: World Bank SABER-WfD Data Collection Instrument 2013.
Note: The scores, ranging from 1 to 4, represent rating of the country's system development in the considered dimensions:
1 stands for latent (absence of good practice), 2 stands for emerging (instances of good practices), 3 stands for established
(systemic good practices), and 4 stands for advanced (attainment of highest global standards). Ratings across dimensions are
assessed by World Bank experts.

Skills for a Modern Ukraine • http://dx.doi.org/10.1596/978-1-4648-0890-6

Ukraine scores relatively well with regard to service delivery, a result of the diversity of nonstate providers active in the training market. Performance of education institutions is weaker in other dimensions, such as providing reliable information on current and emerging skills demanded and monitoring and evaluation of service delivery.

Relaxing Stringent Labor Regulations

Employers see payroll taxes and social security contributions as major constraints to their operation and growth. In 2015 the overwhelming majority of firms in the four sectors surveyed faced problems related to hiring, employing, and firing workers (figure O.7). The biggest problems were high payroll taxes, social security contributions, and wages (high overall and minimum wage). An already large tax wedge on labor increased in 2014–15 as a result of two major changes: Additional taxes for military expenditures were temporarily imposed on personal income, and the tax rate for monthly salaries exceeding 10 minimum salaries (Hrv 12,180) was raised (from 17 percent to 20 percent). These changes increased tax wedges by at least 1 percentage point.

High labor taxation and burdensome labor regulation have prompted employers to evade strict labor regulations by hiring workers informally. Informality has risen steadily since the economic and financial crisis of 2008. Workers hired informally are less likely to be offered training or benefits that allow them to access training. Increased informality therefore undermines the government's goal of making the economy more productive and more competitive.

Figure O.7 Major or Severe Labor-Related Constraints Cited by Ukrainian Firms in Four Key Sectors

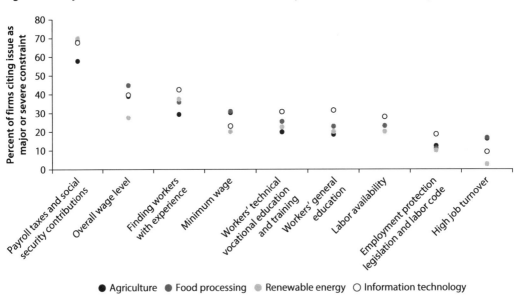

Source: Ukraine STEP Employer Survey 2014.

Figure O.8 Nonlabor Market Issues That Constrain Firm Performance in Ukraine

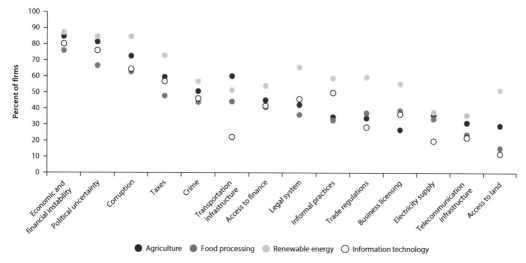

Source: Ukraine STEP Employer Survey 2014.

Key amendments to the labor code made between 2010 and 2015 have made labor relations more restrictive. It discourages firms from increasing formal employment by failing to reduce relatively high labor costs or allowing contracting arrangements that help employers weather business cycles. Instead, it has added new fines, penalties, and restrictions, making it even less attractive for employers to hire.

The efficiency of labor regulations reform would depend greatly on constraining economic and political factors. Most employers report that economic and financial uncertainty, political instability, excessive taxes, corruption, and crime are more of a direct hindrance than labor-related limitations (figure O.8). Employers also judge that capital constraints and competition from the informal sector make it very difficult for many Ukrainian firms to compete.

Policy Agenda for the Modern Workplace

An integrated skills development strategy for employment and productivity in Ukraine should consider three policy pillars:

1. **Build foundational skills for new labor market entrants.** Foundational skills— that is, a solid base in cognitive and socioemotional skills—are imparted largely in early childhood, primary, and lower-secondary education, and play a critical role in the eventual quality of the workforce. Future workers need to acquire good foundational skills to learn better, thrive at school and in the labor market, gain more advanced skills (including technical skills), and be adaptable to rapidly changing labor market needs.

2. **Enhancing the development of advanced skills for current and new workers.** This entails improving the relevance of higher education and training programs (like developing feedback mechanisms between the education-training institutions and firms), setting up incentives to extend the coverage of training programs, and improving the labor market information system for informed decision making.

3. **Improve the institutional environment to ease the use of current workforce's skills.** There are critical institutional factors that facilitate or hinder employment and job creation. These include an institutional environment that enables more hiring, better job matching, and facilitating worker internal mobility. These pillars calls for a set of policy priorities: reforming education and training institutions, reforming the institutional environment, create firm-level incentives to train, and provide assistance to individuals (table O.4).

Pillar 1: Building Foundational Skills for New Labor Market Entrants

The formation of cognitive and socioemotional skills is a multistage process affected by environment and investments. Skills formation is a cumulative process and interventions have to be implemented as an integrated set across one's life. The familial environment (the household's living standards, parents'

Table O.4 Proposed Priorities and Actions for Improving Workforce Skills and Making the Ukrainian Economy More Productive

Priority	Corresponding actions
Reform the institutional environment	• Institutionalize a system that allows providers of education, training, and lifelong learning to identify the skills employers demand and integrate them into sector program curricula. • Reform labor regulations to reduce labor costs, which disincentivize training and job creation.
Reform education and training institutions	• Validate and align education and training curricula with sector employment needs and required industry credentials. • Improve the strategic orientation and oversight of the workforce development system. • Provide career awareness opportunities, starting in secondary school, in partnership with local industry.
Create firm-level incentives to train	• Create systemic partnerships between employers and education and (formal and informal) training institutions. • Offer incentives for on-the-job and off-the-job training and opportunities for apprenticeships, internships, and fellowships, to provide early sector workplace experiences and entrepreneurship. • Evaluate and enhance social security contribution tax rebates to promote job creation and investment in worker skills.
Provide assistance to individuals	• Improve the effectiveness of public employment and training services to facilitate access to jobs, lifelong learning, and skills upgrading opportunities for all workers and training for productive entrepreneurship. • Improve the functioning of employment and training assistance programs to help vulnerable populations (especially internally displaced people and the long-term unemployed) acquire skills relevant to the labor market and become economically active. • Provide financial incentives for skills upgrading and continuous training. • Ease constraints to accessing financing for productive entrepreneurship.

education, and relationships within the family) and home learning environment play a tremendous part in shaping the production of cognitive and socioemotional skills. Marketable skills are developed after childhood through informal learning, formal schooling, training, and on-the-job learning. National institutions such as the health care system and the school system are major components that can alter the cognitive and socioemotional development of an individual. The benefits of an investment depend on an individual's prevailing level of skills.

Interventions for socioemotional learning must target optimal periods for the development of key skills, namely when individuals are biologically and socially ready (Guerra, Modecki, and Cunningham 2014). Primary school-age childhood and adolescence are optimal (but not the only) periods—primary school because that is when children first need to interact with others on their own (parents largely do it when the kids are younger). In adolescence more complex social interactions emerge due to neurobiological changes, larger influence of peer acceptance, and social changes that provide opportunities to develop more complex patterns of social problem solving. The period between the ages of 6 and 11 is optimal for all dimensions of socioemotional skills but younger or older ages are also optimal across dimensions. For example, resilience is best developed from birth through age 11, while ethics is optimally developed between the ages of 6 and 18.

Socioemotional skills can be fostered by a variety of interventions, characterized by specific objectives, targeting age period—preschool, school age, youth, and adult age—and places of implementation such as school, work, or centers. Mentoring, parenting, and human interactions are the unifying themes of successful skills development strategies across the entire life cycle (see Heckman and Mosso 2014 and Kautz and others 2014 for reviews of interventions fostering skills over the life cycle). Early childhood interventions—like those promoting parent-child interactions—offer the largest returns and greatly influence long-term outcomes. For school-age children, a range of countries have implemented system-wide reforms to incorporate socioemotional skills in learning standards and curricula, training not only children but also teachers and school principals. Many early or middle childhood programs also aim to foster cognitive skills. For adolescents, most promising programs integrate aspects of work into traditional education and/or provide mentoring. Extracurricular and after-school programs using arts or sports to teach socioemotional skills are also valuable alternative approaches. Socioemotional skills can also be included in job training programs in additional to technical training, like in the youth training programs implemented in many Latin American countries. Many unknowns remain with regard to the right dose of training of these programs, the sequencing, the focus on single or multiple facets, their long-term impact, quality, design of mechanisms, and incentives. These considerations should be kept in mind to design interventions and integrate them into existing structures.

Pillar 2: Enhancing the Development of Advanced Skills for Current and New Workers

Building a strong leadership structure and adopting performance-based financing are promising ways to improve the quality of the post-secondary education.

To align the Ukrainian system with well-managed workforce development systems around the world, it will be critical for the government to follow through in the following five areas:

- A high-level leadership committee to set the strategic plan and the vision of the workforce development system, to align its policies with the country's socioeconomic goals, and to ensure coordination among stakeholders
- A more effective institutional setup for implementation of the National Qualification Framework (NQF)
- Regular evaluation of the impact and enhancement of existing training programs for all modes of delivery with regard to graduates' labor market outcomes
- Funding linked to enrollments, performance, and effectiveness of training programs
- Fostering competition among vocational education and training (VET) institutions to enhance the provision of quality educational services

A major shift to improve the relevance of postsecondary education is to establish steady links between education institutions and enterprises by setting up standards and adapting curricula. To ensure to train workers with skills that are demanded by employers, postsecondary education institutions should systematize partnerships with organizations in industry to develop occupation standards and adequate curricula and regularly review them. Ideally, the identification and quality review of occupation and skills standards for the workplace would be coordinated by a special government body dedicated to this task. Financial support and technical assistance from local and international partners, donors, and the private sector should be sought to ensure proper implementation and integration of the new standards throughout the education and training system.[2] Occupation standards would help the private sector to play a more active role in curriculum design. As an example, Chicago's college system was fully reformed to align its curricula and activities with the needs of employers. As one of the most important institutions beyond the formal education system that provide opportunities for lifelong learning, the State Employment Services of Ukraine could also tie training and retraining to local labor demands more closely.

Financial incentives for firms could be considered to promote on-the-job training, an effective way for workers and labor market newcomers to build advanced skills. On-the-job training can take various forms such as training for permanent employees or opportunities for apprenticeships, internships, and fellowships for new workers to provide early sector workplace experiences. An employer training investment program that assists interested businesses in training their employees could be targeted at companies looking to expand, hoping to relocate to favorable geographic areas, or in jeopardy of closing. Program participation should be made contingent on criteria that address productivity concerns (such as having clear job creation/retention goals) and have fund-matching mechanisms to prevent abuse. With respect to off-the-job training, short-term work schemes can retrain participants to be better qualified for occupations available in their local labor market.[3] The State Employment Services of Ukraine could act as a bridge between firms or job seekers and training providers by coordinating the design of training, sharing equipment, and establishing teacher-practitioner arrangements, among others. Whatever the setting, the training programs should be carefully monitored and evaluated to ensure their quality.

A better information system on the labor market is essential to facilitate fruitful investments in skills formation and identifying the demand for skills. Students, their families, and job seekers should have access to reliable information on labor market prospects across higher education fields and institutions and job requirements. Career and labor market information that help intervene early in the decision making can prevent misalignments later. Outreach efforts are critical and could include online introduction to education and training programs, classroom speakers, plant tours, and shadowing experiences while in school. A labor market information platform should also contain up-to-date information on skills and occupations in demand for workers and educators and training providers: on job vacancies, their requirements (for instance, with regard to experience, education, or skills), wage information in the sector and occupancy (by personal and geographic characteristics), among other relevant dimensions.[4]

Pillar 3: Improving the Institutional Environment to Ease the Use of Current Workforce's Skills

A strategy to increase the use of people's skills is to encourage job creation through labor regulation reforms while ensuring workers benefit from sufficient social protection. In the Eastern Europe and Central Asia region, Ukraine has a high tax wedge—the difference between the total cost of labor for an employer and the take-home pay that the worker receives. The government of Ukraine should evaluate the effectiveness of social security contribution tax refunds currently in place (since 2013) and where labor costs can be further reduced, for longer-term measures (for a detailed review of policy options to reduce labor costs, see Kuddo 2011). More contractual diversity would also be a lever for job creation by easing the recourse to temporary forms of employment, increasing the length and scope of term contracts, and allowing flexible working hours. However, contract diversity and reduced labor costs should not come at the expense of workers' protection in case of job loss, meaning that the government should shift from the protection of jobs to protection of workers by providing support during periods of transition from one job to another (a model called "flexicurity"). Support can be provided either through income (unemployment insurance) or active labor market programs like retraining.

Promoting the best use of skills also requires efficient intermediation between job seekers and jobs. Efficient labor intermediation services rely on comprehensive information about labor demand, as emphasized in the agenda for pillar 2, but also require to address the full range of constraints faced by a heterogeneous vulnerable population in the labor market (for example, long-term unemployed, youth, informal workers). In this spirit, the State Employment Service could improve its services in developing and using a statistical profiling tool, which can also be used to link individuals to short-term and long-term social assistance for those who are less able to work. Such a tool can help avoid duplication in the provision of services and, in the conflict context, can help in the integration of internally displaced people (IDP) by registering and providing them with labor and social services and also assistance with a focus on activation.

Removing the barriers to internal migration would allow workers to find more job opportunities and make full use of their skills. Ukraine's low internal mobility per international standards is mainly due to the regulatory framework. Ensuring the portability of social benefits across region and removing administrative procedures that require people to be officially registered at their place of residence, although many people prefer not to register a new residence for various reasons, would support internal migration of workers.

Notes

1. The assessment is based on the Systems Approach for Better Education Results (SABER), a World Bank tool that allows countries to document and assess their workforce development policies and institutions.

2. International experience from various countries that have undergone similar reforms or lead in this area (such as Australia, Ireland, the United Kingdom, the Republic of Korea, and Malaysia) should be assessed.

3. Short-term work schemes are not uncommon in Ukraine, but their take-up rate can be increased by not only tying the work activities suited to the education level of the participants (for example, less manual and more intellectual in nature) but also tying the program to occupational retraining which responds to the demands of the local labor market.

4. A methodology tested in this report provides an example of collection of job vacancies and identification of job requirements. This exercise could be pursued and continuously updated by the State Employment Service in partnerships with the local private sector.

References

Almlund, M., A. L. Duckworth, J. J. Heckman, and T. Kautz. 2011. "Personality Psychology and Economics." In *Handbook of the Economics of Education*, Vol. 2, edited by E. A. Hanushek. Amsterdam: North-Holland.

Arias, O. S., C. Sanchez-Paramo, M. E. Davalos, I. Santos, E. R. Tiongson, C. Gruen, N. de Andrade Falcao, G. Saiovici, and C. A. Cancho. 2014. "Back to Work: Growing with Jobs in Europe and Central Asia." Europe and Central Asia Reports. Washington, DC: World Bank.

Banerji, A., W. Cunningham, A. Fiszbein, E. King, H. Patrinos, D. Robalino and J.-P. Tan. 2010. *Stepping Up Skills for More Jobs and Higher Productivity*. Washington, DC: World Bank.

Borghans, L., A. L. Duckworth, J. J. Heckman, and B. ter Weel. 2008. "The Economics and Psychology of Personality Traits." *Journal of Human Resources* 34 (4): 972–1059.

Fields, G. 2003. "Accounting for Income Inequality and Its Change: A New Method, with Application to the Distribution of Earnings in the United States." *Research in Labor Economics* 22:1–38.

Guerra, N., K. Modecki, and W. Cunningham. 2014. "Social-Emotional Skills Development across the Life Span: PRACTICE." World Bank Policy Research Working Paper 7123, Washington, DC: World Bank.

Heckman, J. J., and S. Mosso. 2014. "The Economics of Human Development and Social Mobility." *Annual Review of Economics* 6: 689–733.

Heckman, J. J., J. Stixrud, and S. Urzúa. 2006. "The Effects of Cognitive and Noncognitive Abilities on Labor Market Outcomes and Social Behavior." *Journal of Labor Economics* 24 (3): 411–82.

Kautz, T., J. J. Heckman, R. Diris, B. T. Weel, and L. Borghans. 2014. "Fostering and Measuring Skills: Improving Cognitive and Non-cognitive Skills to Promote Lifetime Success." *OECD Education Working Papers* 110. OECD Publishing.

Kuddo, A. 2011. *International Experience in Reforming Employment Regulations. Technical Assistance to the Government of Ukraine.* Washington, DC: World Bank.

OECD (Organisation for Economic Co-operation and Development). 2015. *Skills for Social Progress: The Power of Social and Emotional Skills.* OECD Skills Studies. Paris: OECD Publishing.

Roberts, B. W. 2009. "Back to the Future: Personality and Assessment and Personality Development." *Journal of Research in Personality* 43 (2): 137–145.

World Bank. 2011. *Ukraine—Equal Access to Quality Education in Ukraine Project.* Washington, DC: World Bank.

———. 2014. *Doing Business 2015: Going Beyond Efficiency.* Washington, DC: World Bank.

CHAPTER 1

Introduction

Skills—the ability to perform tasks and respond to situations—are fundamental to employability and productivity. Providing workers with skills that improve their employability—so that they find good jobs—is a critical policy challenge.

To formulate policy, it is vital to understand how skills are formed and what role they play in the labor market. Focusing on skills development could help Ukraine overcome obstacles in its path to higher productivity and social progress. Equipping people with skills that allow them to grow, learn, and undertake tasks employers demand would make the economy more productive. Creating a more employable and productive workforce would help offset a range of labor-market challenges, including stringent labor regulations, lack of opportunities in some regions, and a rapidly aging population.

Low Productivity and a Shrinking Labor Force

Ukraine has implemented market-oriented reforms since the early 2000s, but its progress lags that of most other countries in Eastern Europe and Central Asia, particularly in institutional and business environment reforms (Arias and others 2014). In June 2014 the World Bank's Doing Business report ranked Ukraine 96th out of 189 economies, partly because of its poor performance on legal processes (such as resolving insolvency and registering property), taxation, and trade costs (World Bank 2014). Ukraine's labor regulations are also holding it back: It is one of only two countries in Eastern Europe and Central Asia that still has a pretransition labor code in effect since 1971, although it has been amended numerous times.

The slow pace of reform adversely affects productivity, which limits economic prosperity. Ukraine's labor productivity level (the value added per input) is among the lowest of all transition economies. Low productivity reduces the country's competitiveness, making it difficult to attract investments and develop economic opportunities.

The country's low level of labor productivity is reflected in the poor allocation of its workforce. Data from the 2013 Ukraine Labor Force Survey indicate that more than half (54 percent) of Ukraine's private sector workforce was employed in low-productivity sectors, such as agriculture, trade, and construction, and a third was employed in industry. Less than 10 percent worked in higher-productivity sectors, such as financial and businesses services or information and communications technology. More than a fifth of workers were informal, meaning they had no written labor contract, were not subject to employment protection legislation, and did not receive social insurance. Almost all informal jobs are low paying, with poor working conditions, unstable employment (by term or duration), and limited training opportunities. Others were underemployed or paid with delays. In addition, 20 percent of people 15–24 and 60 percent of people 55–64 were not working or looking for a job (Kupets 2014).

Low internal mobility—people moving within the country to find jobs—contributes to the weak workforce allocation and limited productivity growth. Labor reallocation across sectors and regions increases both productivity and growth (Koettl and others 2014). But faced with poor employment outcomes, Ukrainian workers rarely change sectors or migrate to regions of the country with higher employment rates and wages. In 2010 Ukraine's migration rate (the number of people who had moved within Ukraine or abroad within the previous five years) was only 4.5 percent—far lower than the rates in France (26.5 percent) or the United Kingdom (15.0 percent). The low rate of mobility reflects rules linked to civil registration, the limited portability of social benefits (despite recent improvements), and weak incentives and opportunities (Koettl and others 2014).

Ukraine has one of the most rapidly aging populations in Europe. This trend exacerbates employment and productivity challenges by reducing the number of people in the labor force and diverting some workers from productivity activities to caregiving. Holding age-specific labor force participation rates constant, the size of the labor force is projected to shrink by more than 39 percent between 2010 and 2060 (Kupets 2014). This diminishing pool of working-age people will put pressure on Ukrainian firms and make it difficult to maintain growth.

The Importance of Skills for Employment and Productivity

Recent empirical research highlights the importance of skills—beyond formal educational achievement—in fostering employment and productivity. While traditional labor economics focused on years of education as the major factor for capturing skills, recent empirical studies find that other competencies and characteristics are often just as and in some cases even more important in determining labor outcomes (Borghans and others 2008; Almlund and others 2011; Kautz and others 2014; OECD 2015).

A better skills development strategy has the potential to improve firms' performance and productivity of the Ukrainian economy. The lack or inadequacy of skills that employers demand makes it difficult for firms to move up value chains, use new technology, and perform efficiently (Banerji and others 2010; Arias and others 2014). Ukrainian employers surveyed for a set of sectoral studies (in sectors such as dairy farming, aviation, and energy) indicated they were unable to recruit workers with adequate technical training and that failure to do so limited their ability to expand to markets with higher quality requirements, such as the European Union (OECD 2012).

While formal educational completion is high in Ukraine, the education and training systems have not been producing skills that are relevant for a changing labor market. The vast majority of the adult population achieves at least upper-secondary education, and almost half has completed tertiary education. Ukraine also performs well on international student assessments such as the Trends in International Mathematics and Science Study (TIMSS), ranking in the same group as high-income countries like Italy, Norway, and Sweden. However, beyond credentials and students' foundational skills, the relevance of workers' education received before the transition, often vocational, and the appropriate time for tracking students into narrow technical vocational education and training (TVET) schools are questionable. There is also a growing recognition of increasing imbalances between the technical training of workers and the actual fast-changing demands of the labor market.

Types and Definition of Skills

Skills are competencies, attitudes, beliefs, and behaviors that are malleable (modifiable) across an individual's development and can be learned and improved through specific programs and policies (Guerra, Modecki, and Cunningham 2014). People develop some skills in school, but schools are not the only places where skills are formed. Other factors, such as family background, work, and extracurricular activities, also affect the skills an individual develops.

Skills are multidimensional. Although a myriad of terms and taxonomies are found in the economics and psychology literature, there is consensus that skills can be divided into three broad overlapping categories of cognitive, socioemotional, and technical skills (figure 1.1). Evidence shows that both categories of cognitive and socioemotional skills are strong predictors of schooling, labor market, and social outcomes in the long term (Borghans and others 2008; Almlund and others 2011; Kautz and others 2014; OECD 2015).

Cognitive skills are defined as intelligence or mental abilities. They include understanding complex ideas, adapting to the environment, learning from experience, engaging in various forms of reasoning, and overcoming obstacles by thinking. Two broad levels can be distinguished: basic and advanced. Basic cognitive skills are foundational skills or basic academic knowledge, such as literacy or numeracy. Advanced cognitive skills involve more complex thinking, such as critical thinking and problem solving (Cattell 1987; Neisser and others 1996).

Socioemotional skills enable individuals to navigate personal and social situations effectively (Guerra, Modecki, and Cunningham 2014). These skills can be categorized on several levels. At the highest level, an individual is characterized by personality traits (such as conscientiousness, perseverance, and emotional stability) that are relatively stable over time. A popular taxonomy is the Big Five model (box 1.1). Also at a high level are beliefs, aspirations, and motivations,

Figure 1.1 Framework for Cognitive, Socioemotional, and Technical Skills

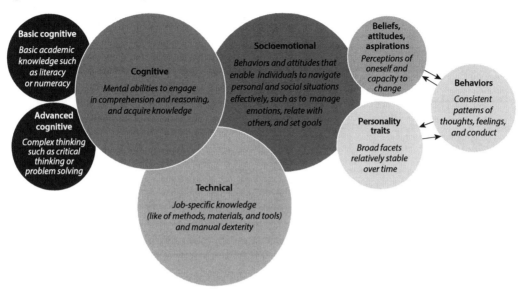

Sources: Borghans and others 2008; Roberts 2009; Almlund and others 2011; OECD 2015.

Box 1.1 Interpreting the Classification of the Big Five Personality Traits

The Big Five personality model is a widely used classification system based on the following traits: openness to experience, conscientiousness, extroversion, agreeableness, and emotional stability (Goldberg 1993; John and Srivastava 1999). These broad traits comprise a range of important facets of personality (table B1.1.1). Some of these facets are strongly correlated with economic outcomes (such as wages), but other facets might have no effect or work in the opposite direction.

Unlike cognitive skills, a higher score on a personality trait is not necessarily more desirable than a lower score. Each trait represents a continuum of individual characteristics that may be

Table B1.1.1 Important Facets of the Big Five Personality Traits

Big Five personality trait	Important facets
Openness to experience	Curiosity, imagination, aesthetics, actions (wide interests), excitability, unconventionality
Conscientiousness	Efficiency, organization, dutifulness, achievement striving, self-discipline, deliberation
Extroversion	Gregariousness, assertiveness, activity, adventurousness, enthusiasm, warmth
Agreeableness	Trust, straightforwardness, altruism, compliance, modesty, sympathy
Emotional stability	Anxiety, irritability, depression, self-consciousness, impulsiveness, vulnerability

Source: Costa and McCrae 1992.

box continues next page

Box 1.1 Interpreting the Classification of the Big Five Personality Traits (continued)

Table B1.1.2 Interpretation of Low and High Scores of Big Five Personality Traits

Big Five personality trait	Low score	High score
Openness to experience	Routine, straightforward	Complex, experimental
Conscientiousness	Spontaneous	Self-disciplined, planned
Extroversion	Energized by internal stimulation	Energized by external stimulation
Agreeableness	Self-interested, suspicious	Kind, willing to compromise
Emotional stability	Anxious, reactive	Resilient, calm

Source: Cunningham, Acosta, and Muller 2016.

beneficial or not depending on one's job (table B1.1.2). Highly conscientious individuals are organized and efficient, for instance, but they may lack spontaneity or flexibility that some jobs require.

---

which influence whether a person believes that his or her intelligence or skills are fixed or can be improved through effort and dedication. At a lower level, they characterize how people think, feel, and conduct themselves consistently (such as managing emotions, working with others, and setting goals) (Borghans and others 2008; Roberts 2009; Almlund and others 2011).[1]

Technical skills are abilities associated with the specialized knowledge needed to perform specific tasks, such as driving a vehicle, operating heavy machinery, programming for the web, or designing objects. Physical abilities and manual dexterity also fall under the category of technical skills (Prada and Urzúa 2014).

Cognition affects the formation of socioemotional skills, for instance, and technical skills can be seen as a subset of cognitive and socioemotional skills (Borghans and others 2008; Almlund and others 2011). It is nevertheless useful to distinguish the three skills sets when designing public policy, because the ways to develop and foster each set are different.

Skills Formation over the Life Cycle

The formation of abilities is a cumulative process that occurs in diverse learning environments. Individuals develop and learn at every stage of the life cycle, from utero and early childhood to adolescence and adulthood. Skills develop progressively, building on previously acquired skills and on new learning investments (Cunha and others 2006). Abilities are partly inherited, but families, schools, other environments, and experiences shape the development of competencies, behaviors, and traits (Heckman 2006).

The early stages of life are critical for the development of basic cognitive and socioemotional abilities. Early childhood environments have enormous impact on later life outcomes (Knudsen and others 2006; Heckman 2008; Almond and Currie 2011; Heckman, Pinto, and Savelyev 2013). Child development, physical and cognitive, during the first 1,000 days of life (from utero to after two years) prepares children to learn later, at school and later at work (Heckman 2004). Deficits or delays in the development of skills in early life can have long-term and often irreversible effects on education, health, and earnings.

Although people who develop skills early tend to achieve more than others, there are key later periods to develop skills, in particular socioemotional skills. Individuals cannot learn any skills at any age. Infants cannot learn to play well with others, because they are not neurologically or socially ready to understand such concepts. New situations emerge as children become adolescents and interact more with peers, preparing them to learn new social processes (Guerra, Modecki, and Cunningham 2014).

The formation of socioemotional and cognitive skills is a multistage process affected by environment and investments. Marketable skills are developed after childhood, through formal schooling, informal learning, training, and on-the-job learning. The health care and school systems are major national institutions that affect individuals' cognitive and socioemotional development.

The benefits of an investment depend on an individual's level of skills (figure 1.2). The familial environment (the household's living standards,

Figure 1.2 Human Development at Each Stage of the Life Cycle and Space for Intervention

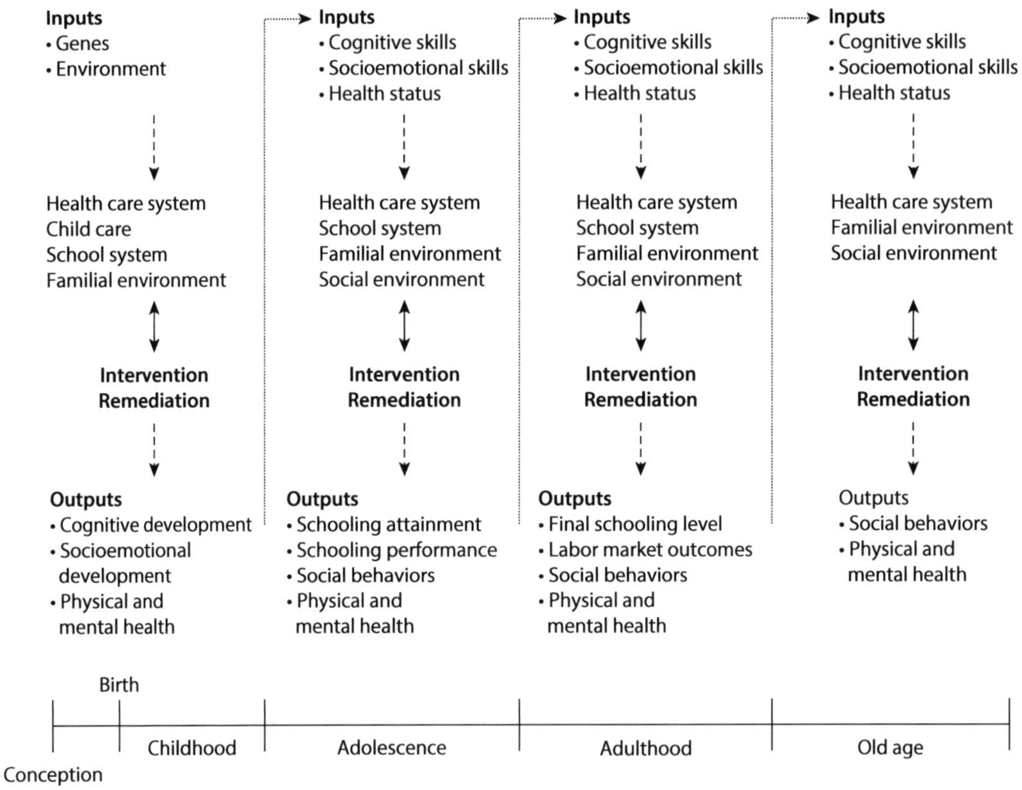

Source: Behrman and Urzúa 2013, fig. 6.2 (p. 125). Reused by permission of Oxford University Press, USA. © Oxford University Press 2013.

parents' education, and relationships within the family) and home learning environment also play important roles in shaping the development of cognitive and socioemotional skills (Carneiro and Heckman 2003; Cunha, Heckman, and Navarro 2005; Carneiro, Crawford, and Goodman 2007). Hostile social environments, such as schools subject to violence and bullying, can have highly detrimental effects on children's capacity to develop traits and behaviors that matter for their success (World Bank 2011; Sarzosa and Urzúa 2015).

Little evidence is available on the development of technical skills. The acquisition of technical skills occurs at the end of adolescence, from secondary education level, after children have developed a foundation in basic cognitive and socioemotional skills. On-the-job training deepens the technical skills acquired in formal education and training and adapts them to the individual workplace (Bodewig and others 2014).

Objectives and Analytical Framework of the Report

Despite the relevance of the skills agenda for employment, productivity, and living standards in Ukraine, there has been little up-to-date or granular evidence to guide policy priorities. To fill this gap, this report investigates the nature of skills valued in Ukraine's labor market, identifies skills shortages, discusses how education and labor institutions affect investment in skills, and proposes practical solutions. The analysis draws on original micro–data sets that allow for a deeper understanding of the distribution of cognitive, socioemotional, and technical skills in Ukraine's working-age population and identifies the skills that employers look for.

The surveys on which the report is based were conducted as part of the World Bank's STEP (Skills toward Employment and Productivity) measurement initiative. The data are comparable across countries in which STEP surveys have been completed, allowing for benchmarking. This study also relies on complementary household and firm surveys, data from electronic job portals, and institutional assessments (figure 1.3).

The analytical framework for this report suggests that skills formation is a function of four key interlinked institutional and incentive factors: labor market institutions, formal education and training institutions, employment and training services, and labor demand and incentives (figure 1.4).[2] (A fifth factor—the broader political and economic context of the country—is outside the scope of this report.) The analysis identifies the main issues that hinder the creation and maintenance of the optimal skills mix.

The report is structured as follows. Chapter 2 examines how cognitive and socioemotional skills relate to labor market outcomes. Chapter 3 presents a firm-level analysis that explores the nature of skills and occupations in demand in Ukraine. It shows how skills and other workforce issues affect firms. Chapter 4 describes the most salient institutional constraints to employment

Figure 1.3 Data Sources for This Study

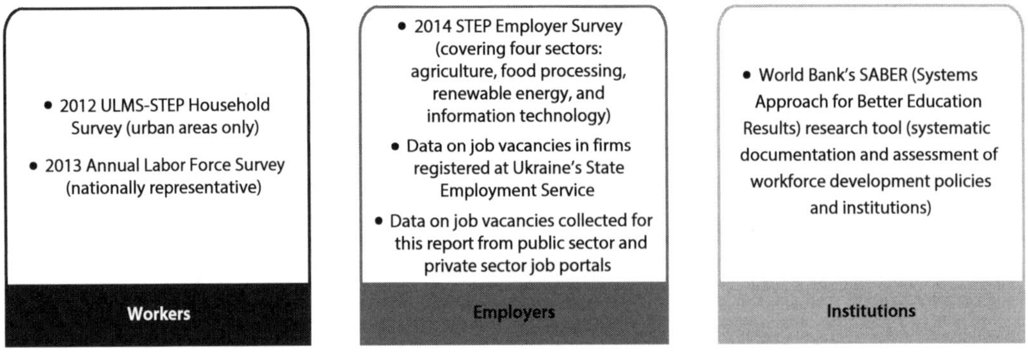

• 2012 ULMS-STEP Household Survey (urban areas only)
• 2013 Annual Labor Force Survey (nationally representative)
Workers
• 2014 STEP Employer Survey (covering four sectors: agriculture, food processing, renewable energy, and information technology)
• Data on job vacancies in firms registered at Ukraine's State Employment Service
• Data on job vacancies collected for this report from public sector and private sector job portals
Employers
• World Bank's SABER (Systems Approach for Better Education Results) research tool (systematic documentation and assessment of workforce development policies and institutions)
Institutions

Figure 1.4 Analytical Framework: Skills Formation as a Function of Institutional and Incentive Factors

Labor market institutions
Employment and training services
Workforce skills
Education and training institutions
Labor demand and firm incentives

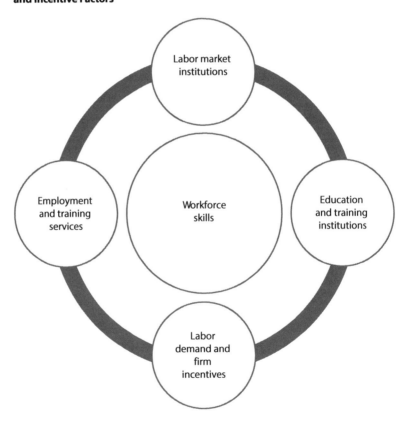

and an adequately skilled workforce, including education, training, and labor regulations. Chapter 5 summarizes the nature of the skills in demand in Ukraine and provides recommendations for improving skills development, employability, and productivity that the government could consider.

Notes

1. In the economics literature, the term *socioemotional skills* is often used interchangeably with terms such as *behavioral skills, life skills, noncognitive skills, character skills,* and *soft skills*. These terms differ slightly. Noncognitive skills and character skills refer to a broad range of behaviors, abilities, and traits that are not induced by intelligence or achievement, although psychologists argue that the characteristics economists intend to capture by use of the term *noncognitive skills* are a result of cognition (Borghans and others 2008). Soft skills and life skills usually cover socioemotional skills such as working with others or managing emotions; they also include more technical skills, such as language fluency and computer literacy (Guerra, Modecki, and Cunningham 2014).

2. This report suggests policy solutions to improve the provision and adequacy of skills of the workforce. Issues related to early childhood development or skills development at lower levels of education are beyond its scope. For this reason, the framework does not include family or environmental contexts.

References

Almlund, M., A. L. Duckworth, J. J. Heckman, and T. Kautz. 2011. "Personality Psychology and Economics." In *Handbook of the Economics of Education*, Vol. 2, edited by E. A. Hanushek. Amsterdam: North-Holland.

Almond, D., and J. Currie. 2011. "Human Capital Development before Age Five." In *Handbook of Labor Economics*, Vol. 4B, edited by O. Ashenfelter and D. Card, 1315–486. Amsterdam: Elsevier.

Arias, O. S., C. Sanchez-Paramo, M. E. Davalos, I. Santos, E. R. Tiongson, C. Gruen, N. de Andrade Falcao, G. Saiovici, and C. A. Cancho. 2014. *Back to Work: Growing with Jobs in Europe and Central Asia*. Washington, DC: World Bank.

Banerji, A., W. Cunningham, A. Fiszbein, E. King, H. Patrinos, D. Robalino, and J.-P. Tan. 2010. *Stepping Up Skills for More Jobs and Higher Productivity*. Washington, DC: World Bank.

Behrman, J. R., and S. Urzúa. 2013. "Economic Perspectives on Some Important Dimensions of Early Childhood Development in Developing Countries." In *Handbook of Early Childhood Development Research and Its Impact on Global Policy*, edited by R. Britto, P. L. Engle, and C. M. Super. Oxford: Oxford University Press.

Bodewig, C., R. Badiani-Magnusson, K. Macdonald, D. Newhouse, and J. Rutkowski. 2014. *Skilling Up Vietnam: Preparing the Workforce for a Modern Market Economy*. Washington, DC: World Bank.

Borghans, L., A. L. Duckworth, J. J. Heckman, and B. ter Weel. 2008. "The Economics and Psychology of Personality Traits." *Journal of Human Resources* 34 (4): 972–1059.

Carneiro, P., and J. J. Heckman. 2003. "Human Capital Policy." In *Inequality in America: What Role for Human Capital Policies?*, edited by J. J. Heckman, A. B. Krueger and B. M. Friedman. Cambridge, MA: MIT Press.

Carneiro, P., C. Crawford, and A. Goodman. 2007. "The Impact of Early Cognitive and Noncognitive Skills on Later Outcomes." CEE DP 92, Centre for the Economics of Education, London School of Economics, London.

Cattell, R. B. 1987. *Intelligence: Its Structure, Growth, and Action*. New York: Elsevier.

Costa, P. T., and R. R. McCrae. 1992. *Revised NEO Personality Inventory (NEO PI-R), NEO Five-Factor Inventory (NEO-FFI)*. Psychological Assessment Resources, Odessa, FL.

Cunha, F., J. J. Heckman, L. Lochner, and D. Masterov. 2006 "Interpreting the Evidence on Life Cycle Skill Formation." In *Handbook of the Economics of Education*, Vol. 1, edited by E. A. Hanushek and F. Welch, 697–812. Amsterdam: North-Holland.

Cunha, F., J. J. Heckman, and S. Navarro. 2005. "Separating Uncertainty from Heterogeneity in Life Cycle Earnings, The 2004 Hicks Lecture." *Oxford Economic Papers* 57 (2): 191–261.

Cunningham, W., P. A. Acosta, and N. Muller. 2016. *Minds and Behaviors at Work: Boosting Socioemotional Skills for Latin America's Workforce*. Directions in Development— Human Development. Washington, DC: World Bank.

Goldberg, L. R. 1993. "The Structure of Phenotypic Personality Traits." *American Psychologist* 48 (1): 26–34.

Guerra, N., K. Modecki, and W. Cunningham. 2014. "Social-Emotional Skills Development across the Life Span: PRACTICE." Policy Research Working Paper 7123, World Bank, Washington, DC.

Heckman, J. J. 2004. "Lessons from the Technology of Skill Formation." *Annals of the New York Academy of Sciences* 1038 (1): 179–200.

———. 2006. "Skill Formation and the Economics of Investing in Disadvantaged Children." *Science* 312 (5782): 1900–02.

———. 2008. "Schools, Skills, and Synapses." *Economic Inquiry* 46 (3): 289–324.

Heckman, J. J., R. Pinto, and P. A. Savelyev. 2013. "Understanding the Mechanisms through Which an Influential Early Childhood Program Boosted Adult Outcomes." *American Economic Review* 103 (6): 1–35.

John, O. P., and S. Srivastava. 1999. "The Big Five Trait Taxonomy: History, Measurement and Theoretical Perspectives." In *Handbook of Personality: Theory and Research*, edited by L. A. Pervin and O. P. John. New York: Guilford Press.

Kautz, T., J. J. Heckman, R. Diris, B. T. Weel, and L. Borghans. 2014. "Fostering and Measuring Skills: Improving Cognitive and Non-Cognitive Skills to Promote Lifetime Success." OECD Education Working Paper 110, Organisation for Economic Co-operation and Development, Paris.

Koettl, J., O. Kupets, A. Olefir, and I. Santos. 2014. "In Search of Opportunities? The Barriers to More Efficient Internal Labor Mobility in Ukraine." *IZA Journal of Labor and Development* 3: 21.

Knudsen, E. I., J. J. Heckman, J. L. Cameron, and J. P. Shonkoff. 2006. "Economic, Neurobiological and Behavioral Perspectives on Building America's Future Workforce." *Proceedings of the National Academy of Sciences of the United States of America (PNAS)* 103 (27): 10155–62.

Kupets, O. 2014. "Labor Market Challenges of an Aging and Shrinking Population in Ukraine." *Comparative Economic Studies* 9: 99–134.

Neisser, U., G. Boodoo, T. J. Bouchard, A. W. Boykin, N. Brody, S. J. Ceci, D. F. Halpern, J. C. Loehlin, R. Perloff, R. J. Sternberg, and S. Urbina. 1996. "Intelligence: Knowns and Unknowns." *American Psychologist* 51 (2): 77–101.

OECD (Organisation for Economic Co-operation and Development). 2012. *Competitiveness and Private Sector Development: Ukraine 2011: Sector Competitiveness Strategy*. Paris: OECD Publishing.

———. 2015. *Skills for Social Progress: The Power of Social and Emotional Skills*. OECD Skills Studies. Paris: OECD Publishing.

Prada, M., and S. Urzúa. 2014. "One Size Does Not Fit All: The Role of Vocational Ability on College Attendance and Labor Market Outcomes." *NBER Working Paper* 20752, National Bureau of Economic Research, Cambridge, MA.

Roberts, B. W. 2009. "Back to the Future: Personality and Assessment and Personality Development." *Journal of Research in Personality* 43 (2): 137–145.

Sarzosa, M., and S. Urzúa. 2015. "Bullying among Teenagers: The Role of Cognitive and Non-cognitive Skills." *NBER Working Paper* 21631, National Bureau of Economic Research, Cambridge, MA.

World Bank. 2011. *Strengthening Skills and Employability in Peru.* Report 61699-PE. Washington DC: World Bank.

———. 2014. *Doing Business 2015: Going Beyond Efficiency.* Washington, DC: World Bank.

CHAPTER 2

Workforce Skills and Their Role in the Labor Market

This chapter examines the importance of the quality of the workforce's skills rather than the quantity of education in Ukraine. Insights from this chapter suggest that Ukrainians from urban areas have good foundational cognitive skills but that Ukrainian employers take these skills for granted and therefore do not reward them. Wages, labor market participation, and occupational status seem to be more closely associated with socioemotional skills, such as being creative, perseverant, disciplined, hardworking, and emotionally stable. The analysis is based on national data and a longitudinal household survey measuring cognitive skills (for a description of the survey instrument, see annex A).

Ukraine's Labor Market

Employment and Labor Force Participation before the Conflict in Eastern Ukraine

Before the onset of the conflict in eastern Ukraine, employment and labor force participation rates in Ukraine were similar to average rates in neighboring European and Central Asian countries. In 2013 the share of working-age (15–64) people that was employed or actively looking for a job was about 68 percent nationally and slightly higher in areas near the subsequent conflict (Dnipropetrovsk, Zaporizhzhya, and Kharkiv oblasts) (figure 2.1).[1] This proportion was higher than in the Western Balkan countries, such as Bosnia and Herzegovina and Croatia, but lower than in most Central Asian countries, such as Azerbaijan and Georgia (Arias and others 2014). Unemployment rates ranged from 6.5 percent in Dnipropetrovsk, Zaporizhzhya, and Kharkiv to 7.3 percent in the Donbas (Donetsk and Luhansk oblasts), the areas that would be directly affected by the conflict the following year. Ukraine had less long-term unemployed than most countries in the region, especially after the 2008 financial crisis (Arias and others 2014).

Figure 2.1 Labor Market Indicators in Ukraine, by Current Conflict Situation, 2013

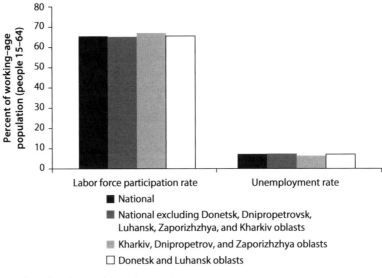

Source: Data from the 2013 Ukraine Labor Force Survey.
Note: Estimates exclude Crimea.

Being employed in Ukraine does not guarantee greater economic stability or welfare: Many Ukrainian workers are informal, employed formally but poorly paid, or employed in low-productivity jobs. According to the State Statistics Service, the informality rate for the population 15–70 was 21.8 percent in 2013.[2] Most informal workers are based in Kyiv.

Ukrainian workers are concentrated in low-productivity economic sectors. More than half (54 percent) of the private sector workforce is in lower-productivity sectors such as agriculture (4 million workers [20 percent of total]). Less than 10 percent are employed in higher-productivity private sector jobs, such as financial and business services, information technology, and professional and technical services. Working in a low-productivity sector is often associated with worse working conditions and lower compensation than provided in high-productivity sectors.

In the Donbas region, which has been directly affected by the conflict, most workers were working for large private firms in the manufacturing, trade, and mining sectors. According to the 2013 Labor Force Survey, 12.8 percent of workers were employed in the extractive and mining sector (the national figure was 3.1 percent). Another feature of the Donbas labor market was the high concentration (60 percent) of workers employed in large firms (firms with 50 employees or more).

Effect of the Conflict and the Economic Downturn on the Labor Market

Employment losses since the beginning of the conflict have been considerable. Formal employment declined significantly between February 2014 and mid-2015 (figure 2.2). Once prosperous manufacturing firms in the Donbas region were severely affected by the conflict and the overall slowdown, with many shutting down. Preliminary figures show that between December 2013 and December 2014 employment declined by almost 40 percent in Donetsk and 70 percent in Luhansk oblast—a loss of about 800,000 jobs in the Donbas region alone (figure 2.3).

Regions near the conflict also experienced reductions in employment. Most job losses were in industry, coal mining, and manufacturing of food products and machinery (figure 2.4). The coal and lignite mining and peat extraction sectors, located almost exclusively in the Donbas region, saw a 52 percent decrease in jobs (136,000 jobs lost) in 2014.[3] Given that a large share of internally displaced people were employed in the extractive and mining sector, there are likely to be misalignments between their skills and the skills needed by employers elsewhere in Ukraine, where mining either does not exist or is less important.

A significant share of employment adjustment took place within firms, through the reduction in working hours, which affected more than 888,000 employees in 2014 (almost 10 percent of all formal employees in Ukraine outside Crimea) (table 2.1).[4] About 49 percent of workers in industry and 34 percent in

Figure 2.2 Number of People Employed by Formal Firms in Ukraine, 2013–15

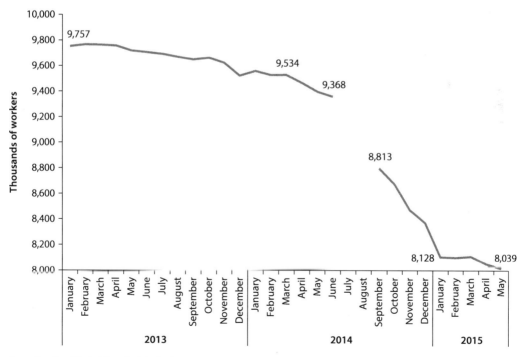

Source: Data from Ukraine's State Statistics Service.
Note: Data refer to legal entities with at least 10 employees. Calculations exclude Crimea. No data were collected in July or August 2014, the peak of the conflict. Data for Donetsk and Luhansk oblasts for September 2014–May 2015 are preliminary.

Skills for a Modern Ukraine • http://dx.doi.org/10.1596/978-1-4648-0890-6

Figure 2.3 Losses in Employment in Ukraine between December 2013 and December 2014, by Oblast

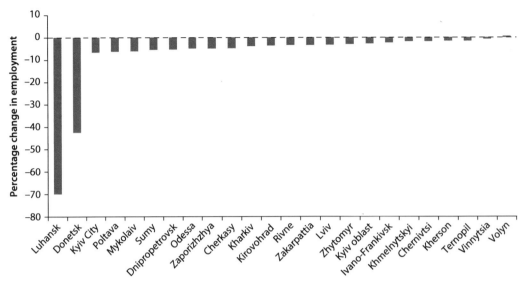

Source: Data from Ukraine's State Statistics Service.
Note: Data refer to legal entities with at least 10 employees. Data for Donetsk and Luhansk oblasts for September–December 2014 are preliminary.

Figure 2.4 Losses in Employment in Ukraine between December 2013 and December 2014, by Industry

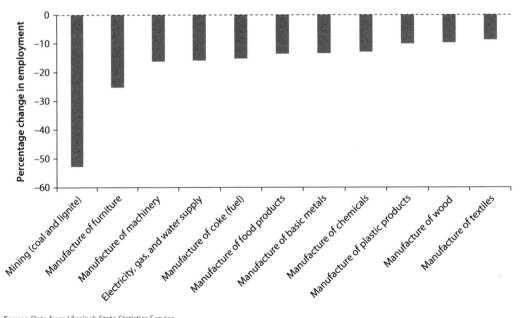

Source: Data from Ukraine's State Statistics Service.
Note: Data refer to legal entities with at least 10 employees. Estimates exclude Crimea after April 2014. Data for Donetsk and Luhansk oblasts for September–December 2014 are preliminary.

the transport and storage sectors worked fewer hours in the first quarter of 2015 than in the last quarter of 2014. The reductions were steepest in the Donbas and neighboring regions.

The conflict and economic downturn in 2014 also affected the labor market through wage arrears. According to the State Statistics Service, total wage arrears (excluding Crimea) increased from Hrv 753 million to Hrv 2,437 million in 2014 (7 percent of the monthly payroll for December 2014). Although this dramatic increase was caused mainly by the accumulation of debt in conflict-affected areas, wage arrears grew in the rest of Ukraine as well (figure 2.5).

After excluding some temporarily occupied territories from statistical coverage in January 2015, the total amount of wages owed (arrears) decreased substantially nationally and in the conflict-affected areas. At the beginning of June 2015, overall wage arrears in Ukraine had fallen to about Hrv 1,811 million (5.4 percent of the payroll for May 2015), with 43 percent of this amount accumulated in two conflict-affected regions. These figures take into account only firms that have reported wage data to the State Statistics Service since mid-2014.

Figure 2.5 Wage Arrears in Ukraine, by Regional Conflict Status, 2013–15

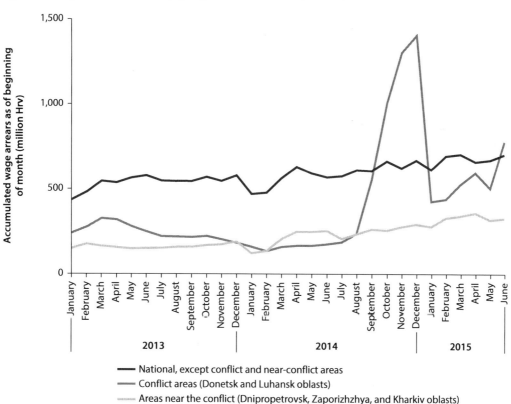

Source: Data from Ukraine's State Statistics Service.
Note: Data refer to legal entities with at least 10 employees. Data do not include Crimea. Data for Donetsk and Luhansk oblasts are preliminary.

Table 2.1 Forced Unpaid Leave and Shortened Working Hours in Ukraine, 2007–15

Year	Unpaid administrative leave		Shortened working hours	
	Number of people (thousands)	Percent of average listed number of employees	Number of people (thousands)	Percent of formal employees
2007	127	1	506	4
2008	180	2	1,206	11
2009	276	3	2,063	19
2010	363	3	1,467	14
2011	190	2	909	9
2012	138	1	737	7
2013	97	1	799	8
2014[a]	91	1	888	10
January– March 2015[a]	48	1	559	7

Source: Data from Ukraine's State Statistics Service.
Note: Data refer to legal entities with at least 10 employees.
a. Data do not include Crimea. Data for Donetsk and Luhansk oblasts are preliminary.

Benchmarking Adults' Skills against Other Countries

The average basic cognitive skills of adults in urban Ukraine are comparable to the average for member countries of the Organisation for Economic Co-operation and Development (OECD) and higher than the average for most middle-income countries. The average level of reading proficiency—the ability to read, process information, evaluate, and use written information—in urban Ukraine is equivalent to the level in Austria, Germany, Ireland, Poland, and the United States (figure 2.6). At this level (2 on a 1–5 scale), adults are able to match text and information, paraphrase, and make low-level inferences (for a description of reading proficiency levels, see table A.2 in appendix A). The average score in urban Ukraine is 269, which corresponds to the upper bound of level 2 of reading proficiency. It is close to level 3, the level at which a reader can understand dense and lengthy written structures, especially complex digital texts, well enough to complete tasks.

Although 269 is far below the average score in high-performing countries such as Japan (296) or Finland (288), it is nevertheless high, especially given Ukraine's income level. The average score in urban Ukraine is significantly higher than scores of urban areas in middle-income countries with lower GDP per capita, such as Armenia or Georgia (see figure 2.6); it is also higher than several high-income countries, including France, Italy, and Spain. (Ukraine's score much likely be much lower if it included the entire population, not just the urban population.)

The proportion of adults who score at each of the five levels of reading proficiency is roughly equivalent in Ukraine and high-income countries: About 47 percent of Ukrainians in urban areas and 51 percent of people in OECD

Figure 2.6 Relationship between Cognitive Skills and Per Capita GDP in Urban Ukraine and Selected Countries, circa 2012

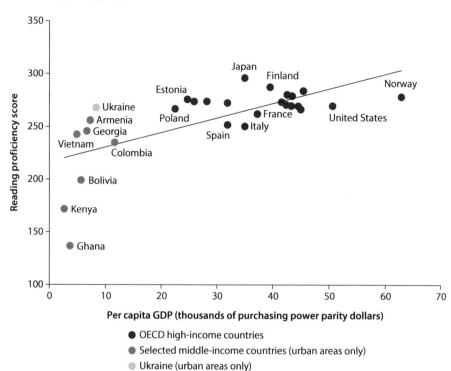

Per capita GDP (thousands of purchasing power parity dollars)

● OECD high-income countries
● Selected middle-income countries (urban areas only)
● Ukraine (urban areas only)

Sources: Armenia, Colombia, Georgia, and Vietnam: STEP Household Surveys 2012–13. Ukraine: ULMS-STEP Household Survey 2012. OECD: Programme for the International Assessment of Adults' Competencies (PIAAC) (2012–13).
Note: Data for middle-income countries (Armenia, Colombia, Georgia, Ukraine, and Vietnam) are representative only of urban areas. Reading proficiency scores range from 0 (lowest) to 500 (highest). OECD 23-country average is 273. For description of reading scores, see table A.2 in appendix A.

countries scored between 3 and 5 on the reading proficiency section of the Programme for the International Assessment of Adults' Competencies (PIAAC) and the Skills toward Employment and Productivity (STEP) Household Surveys. These scores indicate the ability to deal with complex information processing from text. In contrast, the majority of the urban population in comparator countries (72 percent in Armenia, 77 percent in Georgia, and 77 percent in Colombia) scored in the two lowest levels of reading proficiency, indicating that they could identify only simple information from a short text (figure 2.7).

There is a generational gap in basic cognitive skills for adults educated during transition years. The oldest (above age 55) and youngest (below age 35) cohorts of urban Ukrainians have high average levels of cognitive skills. Urban Ukrainians who exited the formal education system more than 30 years ago (people born between 1947 and 1967) score above their peers in urban Armenia, urban Georgia, and OECD countries in reading proficiency (figure 2.8).

Figure 2.7 Average Adult Reading Proficiency Levels in Selected Countries, 2012

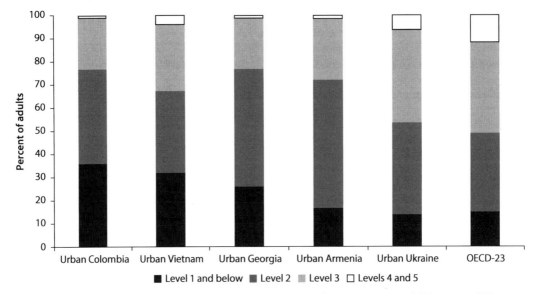

Sources: Armenia, Colombia, Georgia, and Vietnam: STEP Household Surveys 2012–13. Ukraine: ULMS-STEP Household Survey 2012. OECD:
Programme for the International Assessment of Adults' Competencies (PIAAC) (2012–13).
Note: Data for Armenia, Georgia, and Ukraine are for urban areas only. Data for 23 OECD countries (OECD 23) are national. Level 1 and below is lowest
level, 5 is highest. For a description of reading levels, see table A.1 in appendix A.

**Figure 2.8 Average Adult Reading Proficiency Levels in Selected Countries, by
Age Cohort, 2012**

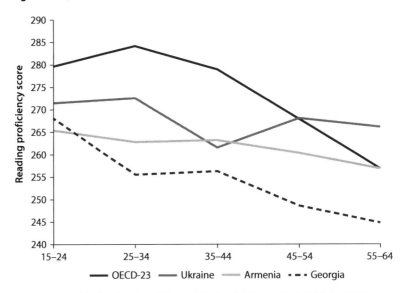

Sources: Armenia, Colombia, Georgia, and Vietnam: STEP Household Surveys 2012–13. Ukraine: ULMS-STEP
Household Survey 2012. OECD: Programme for the International Assessment of Adults' Competencies
(PIAAC) (2012–13).
Note: Data for Armenia, Georgia, and Ukraine are for urban areas only. Data for OECD-23 are national.
Reading proficiency scores range from 0 (lowest) to 500 (highest). For a description of reading scores, see
table A.1 in appendix A.

Figure 2.9 Average Adult Reading Proficiency Levels in Ukraine, by Education Level, 2012

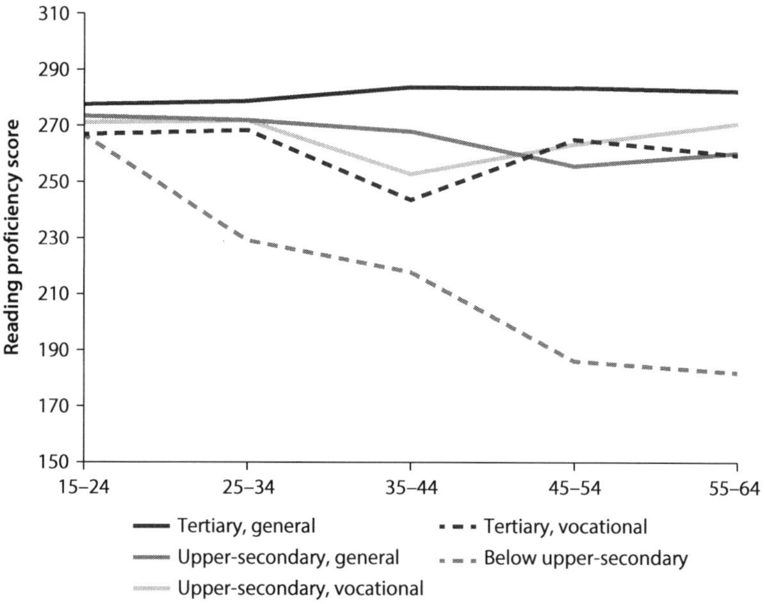

Source: Data from the ULMS-STEP Household Survey 2012.
Note: Reading proficiency scores range from 0 (lowest) to 500 (highest). For a description of reading scores, see table A.1 in appendix A.

Ukrainians who were educated during the transition years (people who were 35–45 in 2014) have the lowest average score among the sample, comparable to urban Armenians and Georgians, a reflection of the poor performance of people with secondary education or less (figure 2.9). Ukrainians born between 1979 and 1999 (people who recently left the education system or are still studying) perform slightly better than other Ukrainians, but these young adults still score below the averages for their peers in the OECD. This *U*-shaped pattern of average levels of reading proficiency—higher scores for the youngest and oldest cohorts, lower scores for middle-aged adults—contrasts with patterns observed in other middle-income and OECD countries covered by comparable surveys, where younger cohorts perform systematically better than older ones (Valerio and others 2015a, 2015b).

Distribution of Skills, by Age, Gender, and Education

There are remarkable similarities in the distribution of reading proficiency across age groups or between men and women (figure 2.10). A notable difference is that older adults (50–64) have significantly lower levels of reading proficiency than youth (15–24) and middle-aged adults (25–49). There are no statistically significant gender differences.

Figure 2.10 Distributions of Reading Proficiency Scores in Ukraine, by Age and Gender, 2012

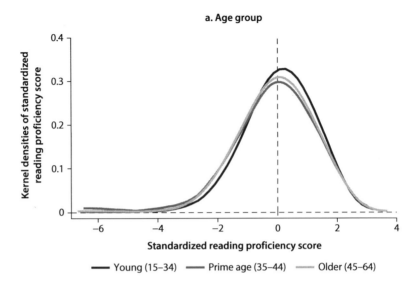

a. Age group

Young (15–34)   Prime age (35–44)   Older (45–64)

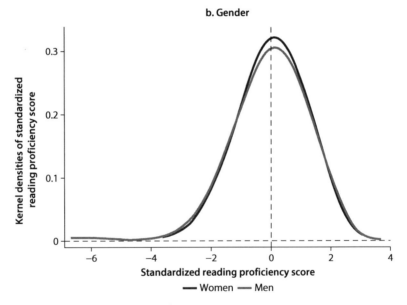

b. Gender

Women   Men

Source: Data from the ULMS-STEP Household Survey 2012.
Note: Differences in the distribution of reading proficiency scores are significant at the 95 percent level for age (but not gender), based on two-sample Kolmogorov-Smirnov tests.

Higher educational attainment does not ensure the acquisition of basic cognitive skills. University graduates have a higher mean score (280) than people with less than upper-secondary education (250), but there is wide dispersion in basic cognitive skills across educational levels, especially at the postsecondary vocational level. The top quartile of general upper-secondary graduates, for example, has higher scores than more than half of university graduates (figure 2.11, panel a). The wide dispersion between vocational post-secondary graduates and university graduates illustrates fundamental differences in training at the two levels (figure 2.11, panel b). The wide variations within education levels may also reflect variation across cohorts (Ukraine's education system may have been less effective in the 1990s than it had been earlier because of transition-specific circumstances, such as lack of educational supplies or payments to teachers).

Small but statistically significant differences between men and women are evident in some socioemotional skills. Women have lower average scores on emotional stability (management of emotions, self-control) but are more extroverted, agreeable, conscientious, and perseverant than men (figure 2.12).

There are very few significant differences in socioemotional skills across age groups (figure 2.13). The biggest difference is that youth (15–24) are significantly less conscientious than older people (25–64). At the same time, they are more open to new experiences, a trait that is fundamental to a person's malleability and ability to be innovative at work.

Figure 2.11 Reading Proficiency Scores in Ukraine, by Educational Level, 2012

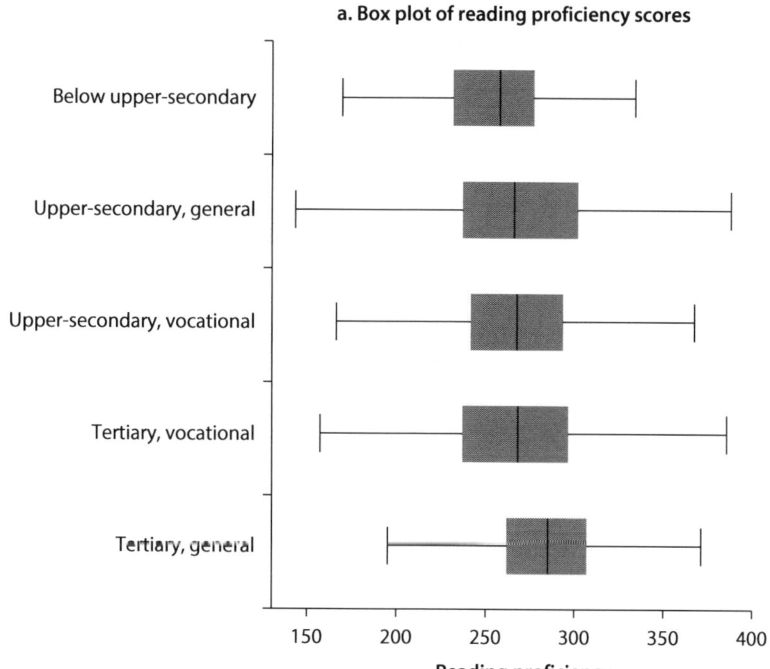

a. Box plot of reading proficiency scores

figure continues next page

Figure 2.11 Reading Proficiency Scores in Ukraine, by Educational Level, 2012
(continued)

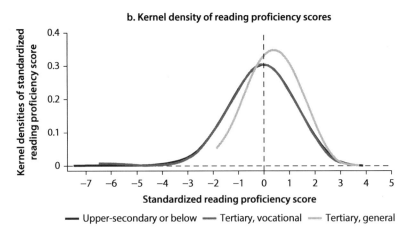

Source: Data from the ULMS-STEP Household Survey 2012.
Note: Reading proficiency scores range from 0 (lowest) to 500 (highest). Panel a excludes outliers.

Figure 2.12 Distribution of Selected Socioemotional Skills in Men and Women in Ukraine, 2012

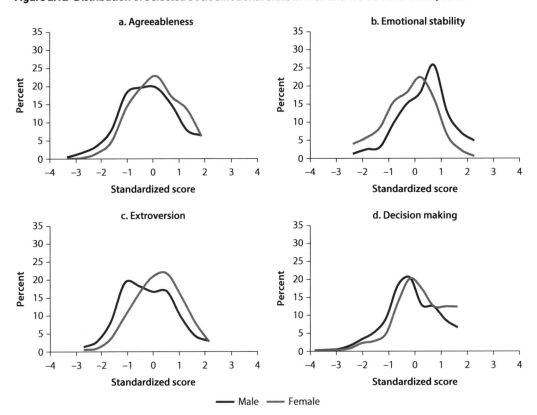

Source: Data from the ULMS-STEP Household Survey 2012.
Note: Differences in the distributions are significant at the 95 percent level, based on Pearson's chi-squared tests.

Figure 2.13 Distributions of Selected Socioemotional Skills across Age Groups in Ukraine, 2012

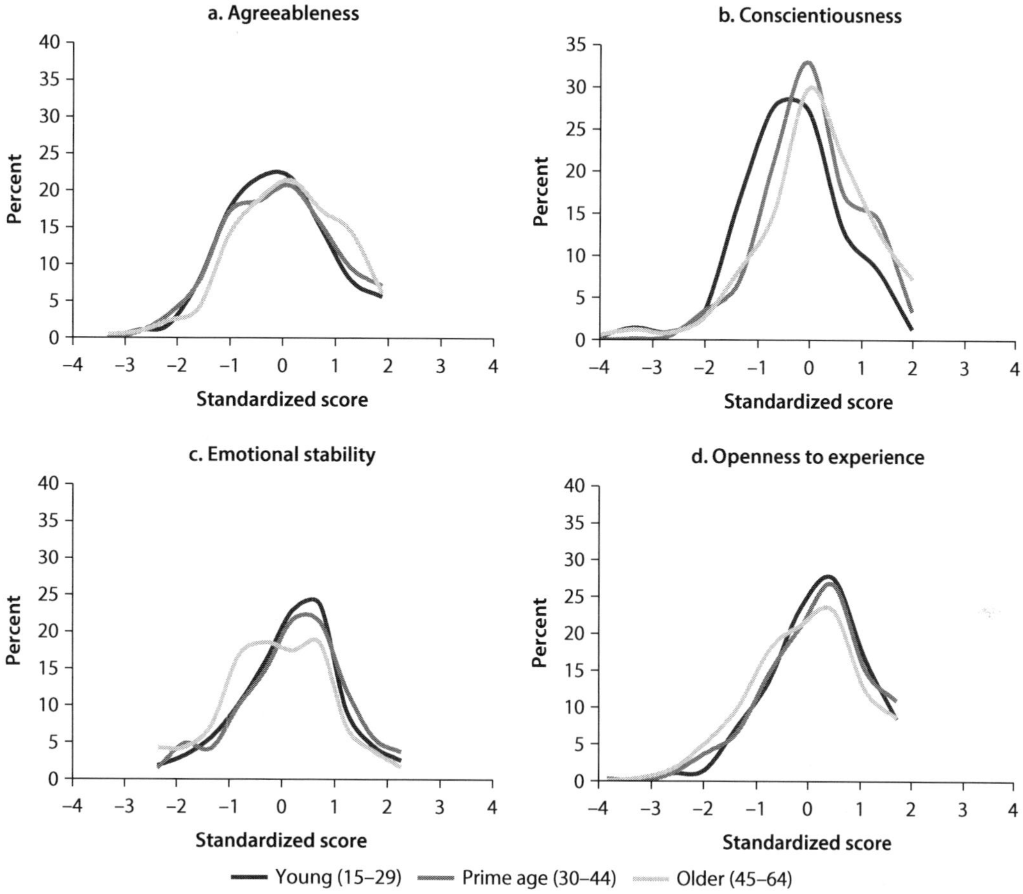

a. Agreeableness

b. Conscientiousness

c. Emotional stability

d. Openness to experience

Young (15–29)   Prime age (30–44)   Older (45–64)

Source: Data from the ULMS-STEP Household Survey 2012.
Note: Differences in the distribution are statistically significant at the 95 percent level between at least two levels, based on Pearson's chi-squared tests performed two levels by two.

Use of Skills at Work

Urban Ukrainian workers use advanced cognitive and socioemotional skills intensively in the workplace: At least 6 out of 10 report using nonroutine cognitive skills such as problem solving, learning new things, and autonomy as part of their regular work (figure 2.14). A similar proportion reports using socioemotional skills in interactions with colleagues and clients even more intensely: Almost half of all workers intensely cooperate with other people, including by participating in regular meetings and interacting for 10–15 minutes at a time with customers, clients, students, or the public.

Most urban Ukrainian workers use information-processing skills at work, albeit often at a lower intensity than technical, advanced cognitive, or socioemotional skills.

Skills for a Modern Ukraine • http://dx.doi.org/10.1596/978-1-4648-0890-6

Figure 2.14 Intensity of Use of Selected Skills at Work in Ukraine, 2012

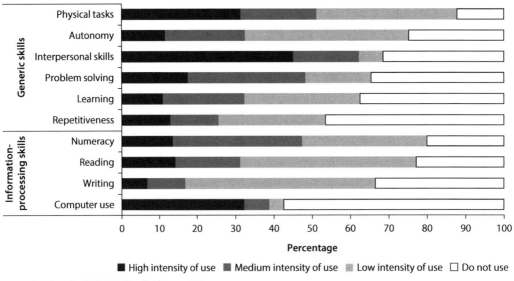

Source: Data from the ULMS-STEP Household Survey 2012.

Figure 2.15 Share of Urban Ukrainians Performing Selected Physical Tasks at Work, 2012

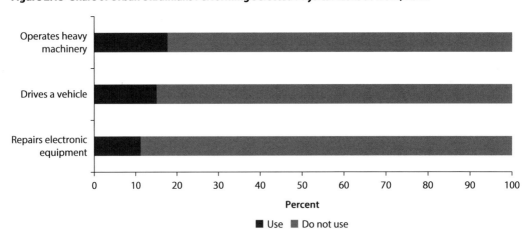

Eight out of ten urban workers use math, but most of them do so only at a low level (measuring sizes, weights, or distances; calculating prices) or a medium level (calculating fractions, decimals, or percentages). Most workers use reading and writing, but most of them do so at a low level.

Less than 20 percent of urban Ukrainian workers performs manual tasks such as operating machinery, driving, or repairing equipment (figure 2.15).

Skills for a Modern Ukraine • http://dx.doi.org/10.1596/978-1-4648-0890-6

Skills That Matter in the Labor Market in Ukraine

The last wave of a longitudinal study, 2012 ULMS-STEP Household Survey, sheds light on how measures of cognitive and socioemotional skills relate to labor market outcomes (Lehmann, Muravyev, and Zimmermann 2012; World Bank 2014; appendix A). The survey covers only the urban population, however; findings are therefore restricted to these areas. Moreover, because skills measures and outcomes are observed simultaneously, the results show only correlations (or associations), not causal effects.

Socioemotional skills are strongly associated with favorable labor market outcomes in urban Ukraine while basic cognitive skills seem to have little influence on these outcomes.[5] Controlling for demographic characteristics, location, and family characteristics, a range of behaviors and personality traits (socioemotional skills) is significantly correlated with participating in the labor market, studying, or earning higher wages. Surprisingly, cognitive skills do not correlate with labor market outcomes and are only weakly associated with being active or studying (table 2.2 and figure 2.16). This finding is in contrast with evidence from high-income countries, where both cognitive and socioemotional skills play important roles in shaping success in the labor market, with cognitive skills more important than socioemotional skills (Heckman, Stixrud, and Urzúa 2006; Carneiro, Crawford, and Goodman 2007; Lindqvist and Vestman 2011). One possible explanation is that urban Ukraine has a fairly high and well-distributed level of basic cognitive skills (as captured by reading proficiency), so that employers evaluate job candidates based on other factors.

Urban Ukrainians who actively participate in the labor market possess a number of key socioemotional skills. People who are more disciplined (conscientious), creative (open to experience), and better at managing their emotions and handling stress (emotionally stable) have a higher probability of being active in the labor market (employed or looking for work) or studying than people who do not possess these traits (figure 2.16, panel a). Counterintuitively, people who perceive others' intents as hostile also have better outcomes, which could be interpreted as the reward for being vigilant and competitive. Being overly cautious about decision making is negatively correlated with employment (figure 2.16, panel b). This finding is consistent with evidence from Germany and the United States, where conscientiousness, extroversion, and emotional stability are associated with labor participation (Barrick and Mount 1991; Heckman, Stixrud, and Urzúa 2006; Wichert and Pohlmeier 2010).

Perseverant and ingenious workers have higher occupational status and wages. Grit and openness to experience are significantly associated with working as a high-skilled professional (such as manager, engineer, or accountant) rather than a low- or middle-skilled worker (such as office clerk, salesperson, or transport worker) (figure 2.16, panel c). These traits, especially grit, are also highly correlated with higher wages (figure 2.16, panel d).

Table 2.2 Associations between Skills Measures and Labor Market Outcomes in Ukraine

		Associated outcomes			
	Skills or trait	Working, looking for job, or studying	Being employed	Hourly labor earnings	Holding a high-skilled occupation
Basic cognitive skills	**Reading proficiency** (ability to understand, evaluate, use, and engage with written text)	Low	*None*	*None*	*None*
Socioemotional skills	**Conscientiousness** (tendency to be organized, responsible, and hardworking)	Medium	High	*None*	*None*
	Openness to experience (appreciation for art, learning, unusual ideas, and variety of experience)	High	High	High	*None*
	Grit (perseverance and passion for long-term goals)	*None*	*None*	High	High
	Emotional stability (predictability and consistency in emotional reactions; absence of rapid mood changes)	Medium	Medium	*None*	*None*
	Hostile attribution bias (tendency to perceive hostile intents in others)	Low	Medium	*None*	*None*
	Decision making (manner in which decision situations are approached)	*None*	Medium (negative)	*None*	*None*
	Agreeableness (tendency to act in cooperative, unselfish manner)	*None*	*None*	*None*	*None*
	Extroversion (sociability, tendency to seek stimulation in company of others, talkativeness)	*None*	*None*	*None*	*None*

Source: Data from the ULMS-STEP Household Survey 2012.
Notes: Associations are based on regression analysis that accounts for all nine measures of skills and controls for demographic and family background variables. Low, medium, and high indicate the size the correlation between skills measures and outcomes (at the 95 percent level of confidence).

Four traits seem to have significant influence on labor outcomes in urban Ukraine:

- Openness to experience: Individuals that are open to experience enjoy learning and are receptive to new ideas. They are more sensitive to art and beauty, need variety, and display intellectual curiosity (McCrae and John 1992). In urban Ukraine highly open individuals are more likely to hold a job and earn higher wages. Openness is also associated with higher wages in the United Kingdom and the United States (Heineck 2011; Mueller and

Figure 2.16 Correlation between Socioemotional Skills and Labor Outcomes in Ukraine, 2012

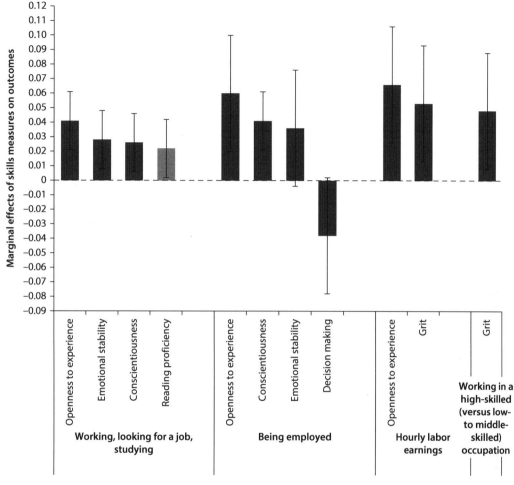

Source: Data from the ULMS-STEP Household Survey 2012.
Note: Orange and blue bars represent cognitive skills and socioemotional skills, respectively. Dots represent average marginal effects of significant skills measures. Lines represent confidence intervals at the 95 percent level. Panels a, b, and d are based on logit regressions; panel c is based on ordinary least squares regression. All regressions are based on nine measures of skills, including cognitive skills (reading proficiency) and socioemotional skills (openness to experience, conscientiousness, extroversion, agreeableness, emotional stability, grit, hostile attribution bias, and decision making). Only coefficients significant at at least the 95 percent level are shown. Measures of skills are standardized. Regressions control for demographic variables (age, age-squared, gender, area of living) and family background (having a spouse, being the parent of a child in the household, number of workers per household member, mother's education, parents' involvement in one's education at the primary level, self-reported economic status at age 15, and number of economic shocks household experienced before individual was 15).

Plug 2006). More flexible, creative, and intellectually oriented workers generally have an advantage in the labor market. Other facets of openness, such as autonomy and nonconformity, may also influence success.

• Conscientiousness and grit: Conscientiousness reflects a range of facets, such as industriousness, self-control, orderliness, responsibility, and conventionality (Roberts 2009). Grit, a trait reflecting perseverance and a passion for long-term goals, is also a facet of conscientiousness (Duckworth and others 2007; Almlund and others 2011). Urban adults in Ukraine with higher levels of measured conscientiousness are more likely to be working, looking for a job, or studying. More perseverant individuals earn higher wages and have higher occupational status, like managers or technicians. The vast majority of studies of high-income countries cite conscientiousness as the strongest predictor of labor and other social outcomes, partly because this trait is useful across a wide range of work-related tasks (Barrick and Mount 1991; Nyhus and Pons 2005; Almlund and others 2011).

- Emotional stability: People with higher emotional stability scores are not easily upset and remain calm in tense situations (John and Srivastava 1999). In Ukraine, people with higher emotional stability are more likely to be employed, looking for a job, or studying. In high-income countries, this trait is correlated with job performance and wages and moderately correlated with employment and participation in the labor market (Bowles, Gintis, and Osborne 2001; Heckman, Stixrud, and Urzúa 2006; Judge and Hurst 2007; Drago 2011).

- Hostile attribution bias: The tendency to perceive hostile intents in others is usually associated with antisocial behavior (Dodge 2003). Surprisingly, in Ukraine it is positively correlated with labor market participation, studying, and employment.

Factors Associated with Variation in Wages

Both people's skill stocks and use of skills at work are associated with variations in labor earnings. Demographic factors markedly contribute to these disparities. Decomposition method helps to quantify how human capital and demographic factors contribute to the total variation in labor earnings across individuals. It complements analyses that estimate the sign, size, and strength of the impact on wages of an increase of one unit of an input variable (like a year of education). This method has been applied to skill surveys of adults in high-income countries and other Eastern European and Central Asian countries (OECD 2014; World Bank 2015).

Disentangling the effects of the stock of skills, the use of skills, and educational attainment on wages is challenging. As educational attainment both increases and is influenced by skills, standard statistical models that simultaneously observe education and skills do not yield reliable results (Cawley, Heckman, and Vytlacil 2001; Heckman, Stixrud, and Urzúa 2006).[6] Similarly, the use of skills at work is associated with individuals' skills stocks. Given these problems, it is necessary to separately analyze the relative contributions of skills stocks, skills use, and educational attainment on earnings.[7]

Urban Ukrainians' stock of cognitive and socioemotional skills explains some wage variations, but demographic and location characteristics play a larger role.

Twenty-five percent of the differences in wages of urban workers can be explained by skills stock, work experience, and demographic factors (figure 2.17, panel a). Socioemotional skills explain 4 percent of wage variation, and reading proficiency accounts for just 1 percent. By contrast, gender explains 10 percent of wage variation (likely accounting for the allocation of men and women in different occupations with different average wages), and place of residence (living in Kyiv or elsewhere) accounts for 5 percent.

Factors associated with wage variation have a distinct importance across age cohorts. For people under 30, work experience is associated with sizable wage differences that are larger than gender- or socioemotional skill–related variations; average work experience is usually limited for people under 30, so the reward for more experience is higher (figure 2.17, panel a). For adults 30–44, gender accounts for 20 percent of wage disparities: Women are overrepresented in low-paid jobs, and a gender-wage gap persists (Kupets 2010; Pignatti 2012). For workers 45–64, socioemotional skills, particularly grit (perseverance) and openness to experience, are associated with the largest wage variation. This finding could indicate that the influence of perseverance and mind openness is accentuated once other factors become less important.

Wage differences across broad occupational categories are also associated with various factors. For high-skilled occupations (such as managers or lawyers), living in the capital, family background, and gender are almost equally important.

Figure 2.17 Factors Associated with Variation in Wages in Urban Ukraine, 2012

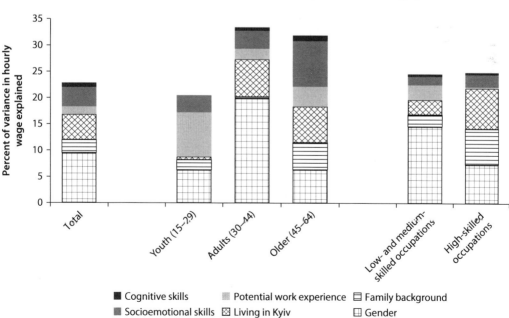

a. Cognitive and socioemotional skills, potential work experience, and demographic characteristics

figure continues next page

Figure 2.17 Factors Associated with Variation in Wages in Urban Ukraine, 2012 *(continued)*

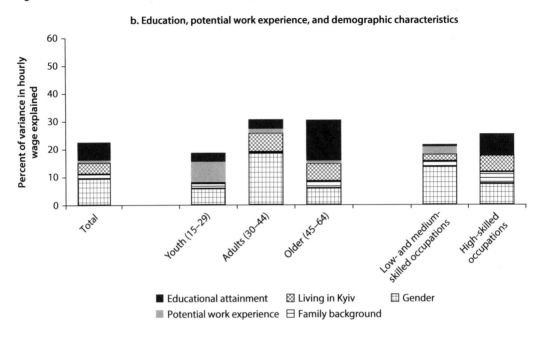

b. Education, potential work experience, and demographic characteristics

■ Educational attainment ⊠ Living in Kyiv ▦ Gender
▦ Potential work experience ▤ Family background

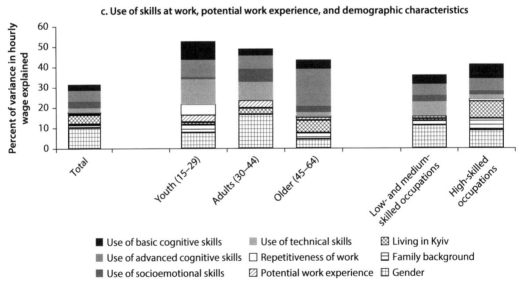

c. Use of skills at work, potential work experience, and demographic characteristics

■ Use of basic cognitive skills   ▤ Use of technical skills   ⊠ Living in Kyiv
▦ Use of advanced cognitive skills   ☐ Repetitiveness of work   ▤ Family background
▦ Use of socioemotional skills   ▨ Potential work experience   ▦ Gender

Source: Data from the ULMS-STEP Household Survey 2012.
Note: Results were obtained using a Fields' regression-based decomposition of the log of hourly wages (Fields 2003). In panels a, b, and c, family background refers to the mother's education and main language spoken at home (Ukrainian, Russian, both, or neither); potential work experience is the difference between the person's age and the approximate age at the end of his or her studies (it also includes a squared term). In panel a, cognitive skills refers to reading proficiency; socioemotional skills refer to openness to experience, conscientiousness, extroversion, emotional stability, grit, hostile attribution bias, and decision making. In panel b, educational attainment includes five levels: below upper-secondary, upper-secondary (general or vocational), and tertiary (general or vocational). In panel c, use of basic cognitive skills refers to use of numeracy, reading, and writing skills at work; use of advanced cognitive skills refers to problem solving, learning, and autonomy at work. Socioemotional skills include interpersonal skills and supervision. Technical skills include driving a vehicle, repairing electronic equipment, and operating heavy machinery at work.

Highly-qualified and higher-paying jobs are disproportionally found in Kyiv. Having parents who are better educated affects the probability of an individual holding a higher occupational status later in life. By contrast, labor earnings of lower- and medium-skilled occupations (such as office clerks and taxi drivers) depend mostly on one's gender, experience, cognitive and socioemotional skills, and place of residence.

Although educational attainment and the buildup of cognitive and socio-emotional skills do not often equate, schooling seems to be roughly associated with wage variation in similar magnitude to skill stocks. When accounting for the highest education completed instead of skills, and with a distinction between general and vocational degrees, education typically captures the wage variation that was explained by both cognitive and socioemotional skills (figure 2.16, panel b).

The type of skills workers use at work explains a larger share of earning differences than either skills stock or education level.[8] Skills used at work, experience, and background characteristics explain slightly more than 30 percent of wage differences; skills stocks and education each account for less than 20 percent (see figure 2.16). Among youth, the use of cognitive, socioemotional, or technical skills at work explains 30 percent of their wages. Technical skills (physical tasks, manipulation of electronics or machinery) and both basic and advanced cognitive skills (such as literacy, numeracy, and problem solving) matter greatly.[9] The repetitiveness of job tasks is inversely correlated with wages among workers this age. The respective effect of the use of cognitive, socioemotional, and technical skills sets in the workplace on wages is similar for middle-age workers. For older workers, the use of technical skills explains more of wage variation (20 percent) than other factors considered.

Notes

1. *Oblast* is the Ukrainian administrative unit corresponding to region.
2. Workers are defined as formal if they hold a written contract, which is usually associated with eligibility for social security benefits.
3. These estimates of employment losses account only for direct changes in employment reported to the State Statistics Service by firms with at least 10 employees. The total number of workers affected is not known. Accurate estimates are difficult to obtain because of widespread informal employment, underemployment, employment in micro-firms, and self-employment.
4. The incidence of unpaid administrative leave—another mechanism firms use to lower labor costs was actually lower in 2013–15 than in previous years, because of strict regulation of its duration and implementation and official clarification by the Ministry of Social Policy to trade unions in September 2013.
5. Since labor outcomes and potential explanatory factors are observed simultaneously, no causal links can firmly be established. Relationships between wages and these factors should thus be interpreted as correlational, net of the effect of a range of other factors.

6. The analysis excludes factors such as occupation type and industry, which are expected to be related to both human capital measures and wages (Becker 1964; Psacharopoulos and Patrinos 2004). It also excludes personal characteristics that could also be influenced by earnings, such as being married.

7. Because wages (the outcome) and potential explanatory factors are observed simultaneously, no causal links can firmly be established. Relationships between wages and these factors should thus be interpreted as correlational, net of the effect of a range of other factors.

8. A study of OECD countries (Quintini 2014) suggests that beyond level of skills and education, the use of skills in the workplace affects wages. Although the methodology does not disentangle causal effects, this finding, if true, would point to the presence of a mismatch between the proficiency of skills and their use at work (for example, people with high reading proficiency not using their reading skills).

9. The difference between the relative importance for wage changes of the stock of socioemotional skills and their use at work could be explained by the fact that very different domains are captured. The survey investigates only whether workers have to interact with clients, colleagues, or the general public and whether they supervise other workers. The socioemotional skill inventory of the 2012 ULMS-STEP Household Survey covers a larger spectrum of facets (see appendix A).

References

Almlund, M., A. L. Duckworth, J. J. Heckman, and T. Kautz. 2011. "Personality Psychology and Economics." In *Handbook of the Economics of Education*, Vol. 2, edited by E. A. Hanushek. Amsterdam: North-Holland.

Arias, O. S., C. Sanchez-Paramo, M. E. Davalos, I. Santos, E. R. Tiongson, C. Gruen, N. de Andrade Falcao, G. Saiovici, and C. A. Cancho. 2014. *Back to Work: Growing with Jobs in Europe and Central Asia*. Washington, DC: World Bank.

Barrick, M. R., and M. K. Mount. 1991. "The Big Five Personality Dimensions and Job Performance: A Meta-Analysis." *Personnel Psychology* 44 (1): 1–26.

Becker, G. S. 1964. *Human Capital: A Theoretical and Empirical Analysis*. New York: National Bureau of Economic Research.

Bowles, S., H. Gintis, and M. Osborne. 2001. "The Determinants of Earnings: A Behavioral Approach." *Journal of Economic Literature* 39 (4): 1137–76.

Carneiro, P., C. Crawford, and A. Goodman. 2007. "The Impact of Early Cognitive and Noncognitive Skills on Later Outcomes." CEE Discussion Paper 92, Centre for the Economics of Education, London School of Economics.

Cawley, J., J. J. Heckman, and E. Vytlacil. 2001. "Three Observations on Wages and Measured Cognitive Ability." *Labour Economics* 8: 419–42.

Dodge, K. A. 2003. "Do Social Information Processing Patterns Mediate Aggressive Behavior?" In *Causes of Conduct Disorder and Juvenile Delinquency*, edited by B. B. Lahey, T. E. Moffitt, and A. Caspi. New York: Guilford Press.

Drago, F. 2011. "Self-Esteem and Earnings." *Journal of Economic Psychology* 32 (3): 480–88.

Duckworth, A., C. Peterson, M. Matthews, and D. Kelly. 2007. "Grit: Perseverance and Passion for Long-Term Goals." *Journal of Personality and Social Psychology* 92 (6): 1087–101.

Fields, G. 2003. "Accounting for Income Inequality and Its Change: A New Method, with Application to the Distribution of Earnings in the United States." *Research in Labor Economics* 22: 1–38.

Heckman, J. J., J. Stixrud, and S. Urzúa. 2006. "The Effects of Cognitive and Noncognitive Abilities on Labor Market Outcomes and Social Behavior." *Journal of Labor Economics* 24 (3): 411–82.

Heineck, G. 2011. "Does It Pay to Be Nice? Personality and Earnings in the U.K." *Industrial and Labor Relations Review* 64 (5): 1020–38.

John, O. P., and S. Srivastava. 1999. "The Big Five Trait Taxonomy: History, Measurement and Theoretical Perspectives." In *Handbook of Personality: Theory and Research*, edited by L. A. Pervin and O. P. John. New York: Guilford Press.

Judge, T. A., and C. Hurst. 2007. "Capitalizing on One's Advantages: Role of Core Self-Evaluations." *Journal of Applied Psychology* 92 (5): 1212–27.

Kupets, O. 2010. *Gender Mainstreaming at the Labour Market of Ukraine and Role of the Public Employment Service*. Kyiv: International Labour Organization.

Lehmann, H., A. Muravyev, and K. F. Zimmermann. 2012. "The Ukrainian Longitudinal Monitoring Survey: Towards a Better Understanding of Labor Markets in Transition." *IZA Journal of Labor and Development* 1 (9).

Lindqvist, E., and R. Vestman. 2011. "The Labor Market Returns to Cognitive and Noncognitive Ability: Evidence from the Swedish Enlistment." *American Economic Journal: Applied Economics* 3 (1): 101–28.

McCrae, R. R., and O. P. John. 1992. "An Introduction to the Five-Factor Model and Its Applications." *Journal of Personality* 60: 175–215.

Mueller, G., and E. J. S. Plug. 2006. "Estimating the Effect of Personality on Male and Female Earnings." *Industrial and Labor Relations Review* 60 (1): 3–22.

Nyhus, E. K., and E. Pons. 2005. "The Effects of Personality on Earnings." *Journal of Economic Psychology* 26: 363–84.

OECD (Organisation for Economic Co-operation and Development). 2014. *OECD Employment Outlook 2014*. Paris: OECD Publishing.

Pignatti, N. 2012. "Gender Wage Gap Dynamics in a Changing Ukraine." *IZA Journal of Labor & Development* 1 (1): 1–44.

Psacharopoulos, G., and H. A. Patrinos. 2004. "Returns to Investment in Education: A Further Update." *Education Economics* 12 (2): 111–34.

Quintini, G. 2014. "Skills at Work: How Skills and Their Use Matter in the Labour Market." OECD Social, Employment and Migration Working Paper 158, OECD Publishing, Paris.

Roberts, B. W. 2009. "Back to the Future: Personality and Assessment and Personality Development." *Journal of Research in Personality* 43 (2): 137–45.

Valerio, A., K. Herrera-Sosa, S. Monroy-Taborda, and D. Chen. 2015a. *Armenia Skills toward Employment and Productivity (STEP) Survey Findings (Urban Areas)*. Washington, DC: World Bank.

———. 2015b. *Georgia Skills toward Employment and Productivity (STEP) Survey Findings (Urban Areas)*. Washington, DC: World Bank.

Wichert, L., and W. Pohlmeier. 2010. "Female Labor Force Participation and the Big Five." *ZEW Discussion Papers* 10-003, Zentrum für Europäische Wirtschaftsforschung (Center for European Economic Research), Mannheim, Germany.

World Bank. 2014. "STEP Skills Measurement Surveys: Innovative Tools for Assessing Skills." Social Protection and Labor Discussion Paper 1421, World Bank, Washington, DC.

———. 2015. *Skills Gaps and the Path to Successful Skills Development: Emerging Findings from Skills Measurement Surveys in Armenia, Georgia, FYR Macedonia, and Ukraine.* Washington, DC: World Bank.

CHAPTER 3

Employer Demand for Skills and Labor

This chapter uses job vacancy data and data from a firm survey to explore the extent to which skills are a constraint for firms in Ukraine and identify the occupations and nature of the skills most in demand. It provides in-depth information on labor demand, skills requirements, and training practices in four key sectors: agriculture, food processing, renewable energy, and information technology (IT) (box 3.1). (For a description of the Ukraine Skills toward Employment and Productivity [STEP] Employer Survey, see appendix B).

Skills as a Binding Constraint for Firms in Ukraine

The lack or mismatch of skills of firms' employees can prevent firms from achieving their business objectives. Firms also face challenges in hiring new workers, because many prospective employees do not meet their skills requirements.

In the four sectors surveyed, 38 percent of firms report that skills gaps prevent them from achieving their business objectives. The figure is even higher in the food-processing and IT sectors, where almost half of firms cite skills gaps (figure 3.1). Lack of skills is less evident in the renewable energy and agriculture sectors, but it still affects at least 20 percent of enterprises in those sectors.

Skills gaps have harmful effects on the performance of firms across sectors. In the IT sector, the problem limits firms' efficiency, service quality, and ability to retain and grow their client base; about a third of firms surveyed report that it also limits innovation (figure 3.2). In agriculture and food processing, skills gaps affect efficiency and increase wastage. Skills gaps have less harmful effects on the performance of renewable energy firms, but as many as 15 percent of firms there report problems associated with skills gaps. Not having a workforce with the right skills in key economic sectors such as IT and food processing—which encompass a wide range of occupational levels—limits firms' productivity and growth potential.

Box 3.1 Description of the Four Sectors Covered by the 2014 Ukraine STEP Employer Survey

The 2014 Ukraine STEP Employer Survey covers four sectors with strong economic and employment potential (table B3.1.1). They were selected on the basis of their potential for growth, job creation, and ability to attract investment according to the OECD's Ukraine Sector Competitiveness Review (OECD 2012), following extensive consultations with stakeholders.

Firms surveyed are located throughout Ukraine but are concentrated in the Kyiv Oblast and City (except agriculture), the eastern regions near the Donbas region (except renewable energy), and Lviv (in the western part of Ukraine, near the Polish border) (map B3.1.1).

Table B3.1.1 Description of the Four Sectors Covered by the 2014 Ukraine STEP Employer Survey

Sector	Types of enterprises
Agriculture	Crop and animal farms
Food processing	Manufacturers of food products and beverages
Renewable energy	Producers of electricity from renewable sources (water, wind, solar, biomass, and biogas) that are registered by the national commission of electricity and gas market regulation. Sector also includes Ukraine's state company's hydroelectric power stations (Ukrhydroenergo), which administer hydropower plants along the Dnieper and Dniester rivers.
Information technology	Computer programming, consulting, related activities (such as administration of computer equipment), and other activities in IT and computer systems

Map B3.1.1 Number of Firms, by Sector and Oblast, 2014

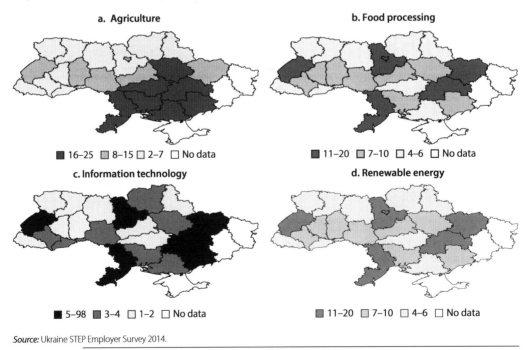

a. Agriculture

■ 16–25 ■ 8–15 □ 2–7 □ No data

b. Food processing

■ 11–20 ■ 7–10 □ 4–6 □ No data

c. Information technology

■ 5–98 ■ 3–4 □ 1–2 □ No data

d. Renewable energy

■ 11–20 ■ 7–10 □ 4–6 □ No data

Source: Ukraine STEP Employer Survey 2014.

box continues next page

Box 3.1 Description of the Four Sectors Covered by the 2014 Ukraine STEP Employer Survey *(continued)*

Figure B3.1.1 Composition of Workforce of Firms Covered by the 2014 Ukraine STEP Employer Survey

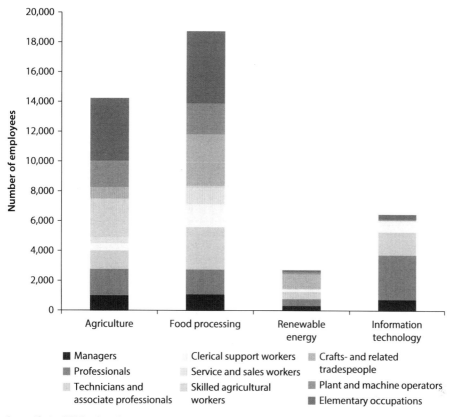

Source: Ukraine STEP Employer Survey 2014.
Note: Shades of orange indicate low- and middle-skilled occupations. Shades of blue indicate high-skilled occupations.

The education and skills levels required in the four sectors vary widely (figure B3.1.1). The vast majority of workers in the IT sector are high-skilled workers (managers, professionals, technicians) with at least postsecondary education. In the renewable energy sector, almost half of the workforce is employed in high-skilled occupations. In the other two sectors, the percentage of high-skilled workers is substantially lower (less than 30 percent). The renewable energy sector has the most diversified profile of workers, with roughly equal shares of high, medium-, and low-skilled occupations. All of these sectors make limited use of common medium-skills occupational categories, such as office clerks and salespeople. These occupations are likely to be more prevalent in other sectors.

Figure 3.1 Skills Gaps Cited by Ukrainian Firms in Four Key Sectors

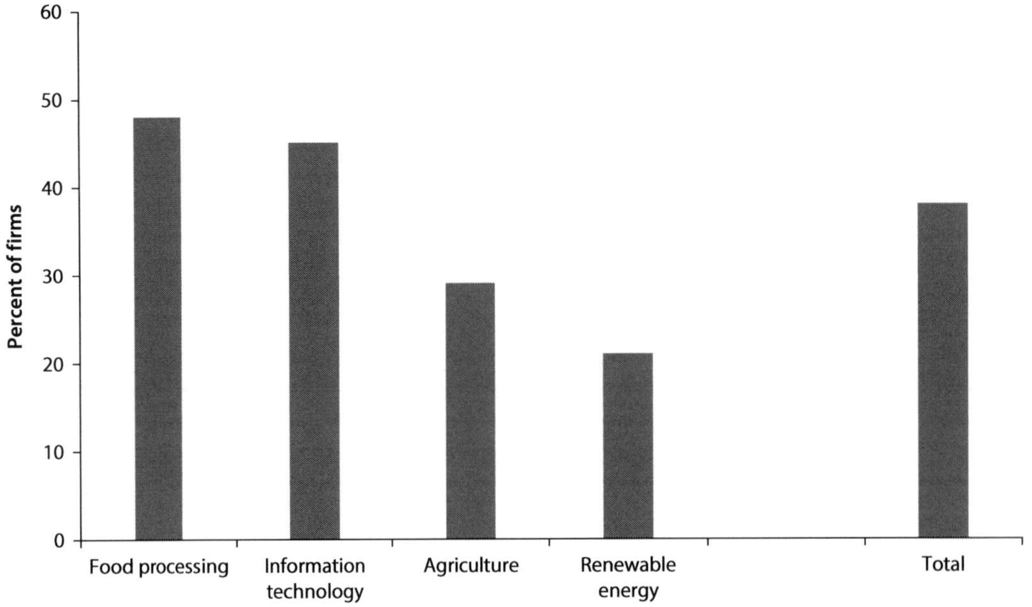

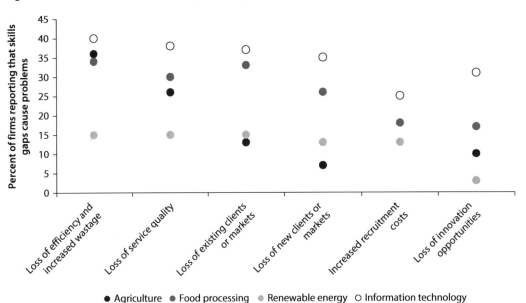

Source: Ukraine STEP Employer Survey 2014.
Note: Figure shows percent of firms reporting significant skills gaps between type of skills employees have and the type of skills the firm needs to achieve its business objectives.

Figure 3.2 Problems Related to Skills Gaps Cited by Ukrainian Firms in Four Key Sectors

Source: Ukraine STEP Employer Survey 2014.

Many firms report that skills deficiencies are the most important constraint to hiring. The proportion of firms claiming that applicants lack the required skills is highest for higher-skilled occupations, at more than 30 percent (figure 3.3). For lower-skilled occupations, other issues, such as wage expectations, constrain hiring. Other labor-related constraints to operate their business include payroll taxes and social security contributions (figure 3.4).

The largest skills gaps in the four sectors tend to be in low- and middle-skilled occupations. In the agriculture and food processing sectors, the largest skills gaps are among laborers (workers with no qualifications) (table 3.1). The vast majority of firms in these sectors (86 percent in food processing and 56 percent in agriculture) face difficulty achieving their work objectives because of skills gap in these occupations. In the renewable energy sector, all firms report large skills gaps in machine operator jobs. Computer assistants and computer programmers are the two categories in which more than 60 percent of firms in the IT sector report skills gaps (box 3.2).

The list of occupations with the largest skills gaps can help guide job seekers. It can also help Ukraine's public employment services align their retraining services with careers in high demand. For example, shortages of bakers in the food-processing sector, repair specialists in the agriculture sector, and sales representatives in the IT and food-processing sectors may be easy to address with short-term training courses.

Figure 3.3 Hiring Problems Cited by Ukrainian Firms in Four Key Sectors, by Occupation Type

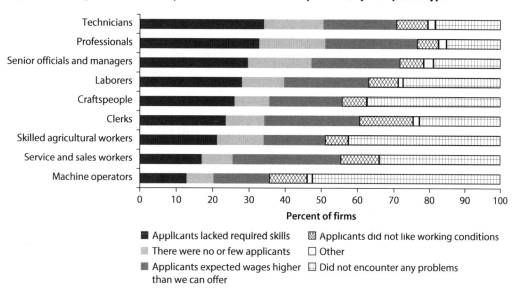

Source: Ukraine STEP Employer Survey 2014.
Note: The four sectors are agriculture, food processing, renewable energy, and information technology. Other includes insufficient work experience, inability to cope with the work, and unwillingness to work.

Figure 3.4 Major or Severe Labor-Related Constraints Cited by Ukrainian Firms in Four Key Sectors

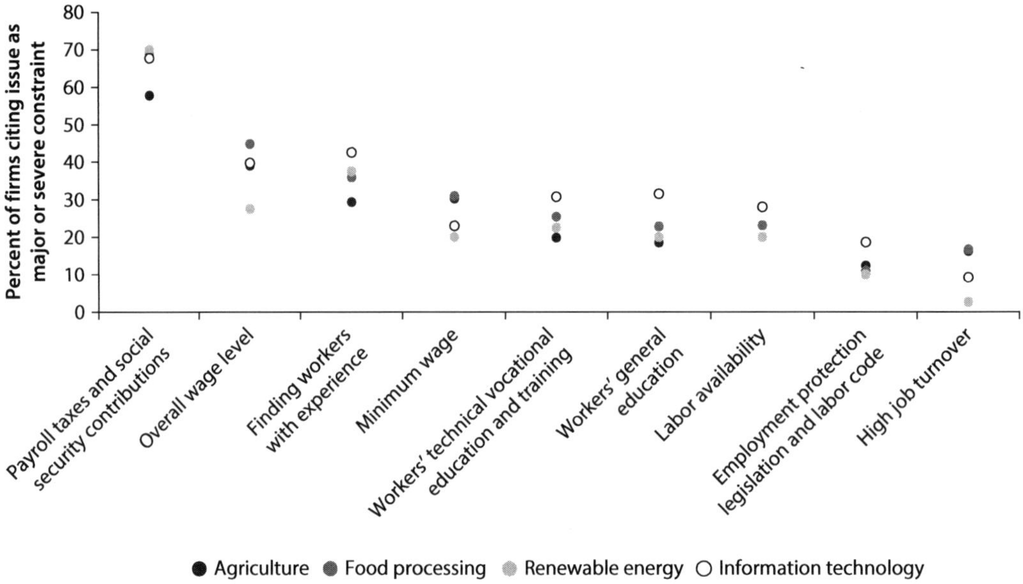

● Agriculture ● Food processing ● Renewable energy ○ Information technology

Source: Ukraine STEP Employer Survey 2014.

Table 3.1 Occupations in Four Key Sectors in Ukraine with Largest Skills Gaps

Sector	Ranking	Type of occupation	Occupation	Percent of firms citing large skills gap
Agriculture	1	Low- and medium-skilled	Laborers	56
	2	Low- and medium-skilled	Tractor drivers	34
	3	Low- and medium-skilled	Animal producers and related workers	30
	4	Low- and medium-skilled	Repairmen	29
	5	High-skilled	Veterinarians	28
Food processing	1	Low- and medium-skilled	Laborers	86
	2	Low- and medium-skilled	Service workers and shop and market sales workers	77
	3	High-skilled	Associate professionals in food technology	57
	4	Low- and medium-skilled	Bakers, pastry cooks, and confectionary makers	49
	5	Low- and medium-skilled	Shop assistants	49
Renewable energy	1	Low- and medium-skilled	Machine operators	100
	2	High-skilled	Cartographers and surveyors	73
	3	High-skilled	Civil engineers	67
	4	High-skilled	Geologists and geophysicists	56
	5	High-skilled	Technology guide bioenergy installers	56

table continues next page

Table 3.1 Occupations in Four Key Sectors in Ukraine with Largest Skills Gaps *(continued)*

Sector	Ranking	Type of occupation	Occupation	Percent of firms citing large skills gap
Information technology	1	High-skilled	Computer assistants	70
	2	High-skilled	Programmers	64
	3	Low- and medium-skilled	Service workers and shop and market sales workers	63
	4	High-skilled	Computer systems designers and analysts	62
	5	Low- and medium-skilled	Clerks	59

Source: Ukraine STEP Employer Survey 2014.

Box 3.2 Why Do IT Firms in Ukraine Decry the Lack of Skills?

According the 2014 STEP Employer Survey, about four firms out of ten in Ukraine's four key sectors—agriculture, food processing, renewable energy, and information technology (IT)—report that skill gaps of their employees prevent them from achieving business objectives. This is even more pronounced in the IT sector, for which more than 60 percent of employers claim that skills gaps of high-skilled job positions, such as computer assistants and programmers, hinder business activities.

Paradoxically, data from one of the largest platforms of online freelancing jobs show that Ukraine is one of the top 10 countries in the world with regard to the supply of IT specialists (figure B3.2.1). Moreover, the large numbers of Ukrainians participating in online freelance platforms are not limited to those with IT skills. They are also among the top suppliers of online talent in design, finance, writing, and legal services.

Are online freelancers underqualified for the needs of Ukrainian firms? A deeper look at the data suggests that the answer is no. Online freelance jobs tend to include very diverse tasks—from microworkers requiring only basic computer knowledge to other positions requiring high computing skills. Yet, many IT specialists working as online freelancers in Ukraine tend to be highly skilled individuals, offering their time to develop programs or provide solutions in state-of-the-art computer languages. Moreover, their earnings—which may proxy their productivity—are very high when compared to the domestic minimum wage. The monthly earnings of the average online freelancer from Ukraine are equivalent to about 18 times the minimum wage (figure B3.2.2). Finally, IT online freelancers do not tend to work for traditional businesses of low-productivity countries. In fact, most of the employers in online freelance platforms come from the most advanced economies in the world, who are looking to recruit cheaper talent abroad.

Given the large number of IT specialists in Ukraine, why do firms complain about the lack of advanced IT skills? The answer is not obvious, but it seems to rely on some deep-rooted issues of the Ukrainian labor market. A first hypothesis could be that Ukrainian firms exhibit low productivity and thereby are unable to offer high enough wages. In fact, labor productivity in Ukraine is 20–50 percent that of other developing economies in Europe and Central Asia

box continued next page

Box 3.2 Why Do IT Firms in Ukraine Decry the Lack of Skills? *(continued)*

Figure B3.2.1 World's Top 25 Suppliers of ICT Workforce

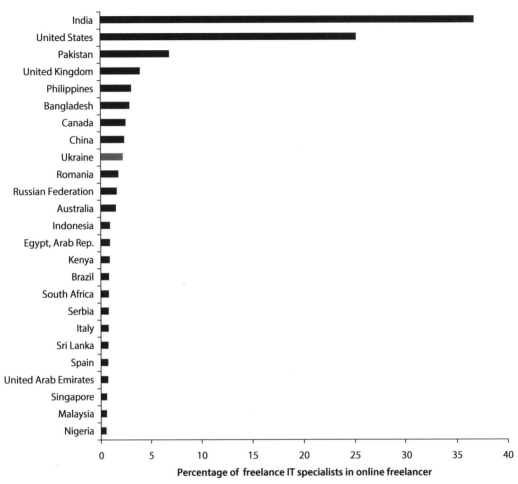

Source: World Bank (forthcoming) based on data from elance.com.
Note: ICT = information and communication technology; IT = information technology.

(figure B3.2.3). Another piece of suggestive evidence of the relative obsolescence of Ukrainian firms comes from a platform of online freelancing. While there seems to be a large supply of online workers from Ukraine, the demand for online workers by Ukrainian firms is very low, as Ukraine is far from the top 25 countries hiring online. That is, while local firms have the possibility to use online platforms to find the specialized computer skills that they need, they do not seem to find this channel as a good option to overcome the skills mismatches and shortages at the current wage levels.

Another reason that could explain this paradox is that rigid labor regulations may also be discouraging Ukrainian IT workers from accepting jobs at home. According to this argument, high levels of employer contributions may create obstacles for firms to attract

box continues next page

Box 3.2 Why Do IT Firms in Ukraine Decry the Lack of Skills? *(continued)*

Figure B3.2.2 Premium for Online Freelancers' Skills around the World

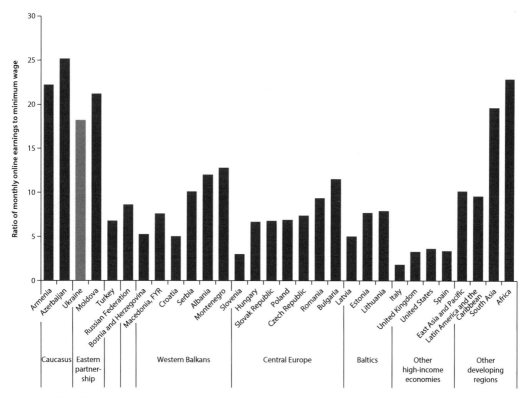

Source: World Bank (forthcoming) based on data from elance.com.

workers given that only a small fraction of the wage bill goes directly to them. Accordingly, difficulty to hire workers on temporary contracts may create incentives for individuals to search for more flexible job opportunities online. Even if firms' productivity levels were higher, labor market regulations might make it more attractive for IT workers to seek online employment.

The characteristics of the job arrangements of online workers in the region could be a reflection of the negative effects that rigid labor laws have on the creation of formal jobs at home. Most of the online freelancers in the region seem to rely on informal or semi-formal agreements to carry out their projects. A survey of online freelancers covering mostly Russian and Ukrainian workers shows that only 11.6 percent of them have an official contract with their employers (figure B3.2.4). The Internet economy may shift the traditional view of the informal worker in Eastern Europe from the unskilled farmer without a contract or social contributions toward one of high-skilled individuals who work informally online.

box continues next page

Box 3.2 Why Do IT Firms in Ukraine Decry the Lack of Skills? *(continued)*

Figure B3.2.3 Labor Productivity in Ukraine

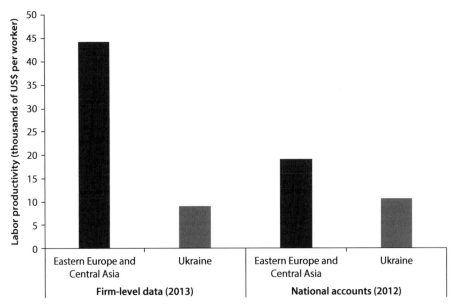

Source: World Bank (forthcoming) based on Business Environment and Enterprise Performance Survey and World Development Indicators.
Note: Labor productivity is defined as sales per employee, and as value added per worker using firm-level and national accounts data, respectively.

Figure B3.2.4 Forms of Agreement with Clients of Online Workers in Eastern Europe, 2012

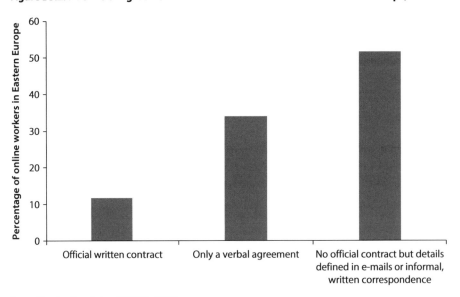

Source: Based on Shevchuk and Strebkov (2012).
Note: The survey includes online workers from Eastern Europe and Central Asia, mainly from Russia (70 percent) and Ukraine (11 percent).

box continues next page

Box 3.2 Why Do IT Firms in Ukraine Decry the Lack of Skills? *(continued)*

Labor regulations in Ukraine have to become more flexible to adapt to international standards; they also need to adapt to the new rules of the game in the Internet economy. The costs of not doing so may include increasing skills' shortages and mismatches and the level of informality in the economy.

What Kinds of Skills Do Ukrainian Employers Seek?

The skills that employers rank as most important are similar across the sectors and occupations examined. Firms in all four sectors cite job-specific technical skills first (technical skills include a wide range of skills, so this agglomeration may inflate the importance of technical skills) (table 3.2). Employers also value a mix of socioemotional skills and advanced cognitive skills (advanced mental tasks, as opposed to basic academic achievements), consistently with international evidence (Cunningham and Villaseñor 2016). Employers particularly value professionalism, the ability to work independently, and the ability to work as part of a team, especially for lower-skilled occupations. Problem solving, communication, and critical thinking are also highly valued, especially in the renewable energy and IT sectors (table 3.3).

The top 10 most-valued skills in the four sectors are as follows:

1. Job-specific technical skills
2. Professional behavior
3. Problem solving
4. Ability to work independently
5. Teamwork
6. Leadership
7. Communication
8. Creative and critical thinking
9. Time management
10. Knowledge of a foreign language

The most highly valued personality traits are conscientiousness (doing a thorough job, being hardworking, and doing things efficiently) and emotional stability (handling stress well, not worrying or getting nervous easily) (figure 3.5 and table 3.4). High demand for these skills is consistent with the fact that these traits are rewarded in the labor market (see chapter 2). Openness to experience (originality, coming up with new ideas, having an active imagination), which is ranked fourth in these sectors, is also highly associated with favorable labor market outcomes (see chapter 2). The specific occupational and sectoral structure of the firms surveyed may explain the difference between these results and the results from the survey of urban households.

Table 3.2 Ranking of Importance of Skills by Ukrainian Firms in Four Key Sectors, by Skills Level of Occupation

Skill set	Skill	Occupation type		
		High-skilled	Low- and medium-skilled	All
Technical	Job-specific technical skills	Very High	Very High	Very High
	Professional behavior	High	High	High
Socioemotional	Ability to work independently	Medium	High	High
	Teamwork	Medium	High	High
	Leadership	Medium	Medium	Medium
Advanced cognitive	Problem solving	High	High	High
	Communication	Medium	Medium	Medium
	Creative and critical thinking	Medium	Medium	Medium
	Time management	Low	Medium	Medium
	Literacy in another foreign language	Low	Low	Low
	Literacy in English	Low	Low	Low
Basic cognitive	Numeracy	Medium	Low	Medium
	Literacy in Ukrainian or Russian	Low	Low	Low

Source: Ukraine STEP Employer Survey 2014.
Note: The four sectors are agriculture, food processing, renewable energy, and information technology. The importance of skills is identified by employers' ranking of the top five skills they consider in deciding whether to retain an employee following the initial probation period. The classification into low (0), medium (1–2), high (2–3), and very high (more than 3) is based on the average index of importance by occupation type.

Table 3.3 Ranking of Importance of Skills by Ukrainian Firms in Four Key Sectors

Ranking	Agriculture	Food processing	Renewable energy	Information technology
1	Job-specific technical skills	Job-specific technical skills	Job-specific technical skills	Job-specific technical skills
2	Professional behavior	Professional behavior	Problem solving	Problem solving
3	Problem solving	Problem solving	Creative and critical thinking	Professional behavior
4	Ability to work independently	Teamwork	Professional behavior	Ability to work independently
5	Teamwork	Ability to work independently	Teamwork	Teamwork

Technical skills
Socioemotional skills
Advanced cognitive skills

Source: Ukraine STEP Employer Survey 2014.
Note: The importance of skills is identified by the employers' ranking from 1 to 5 of the top five skills of employees on probation period to be retained.

The importance of socioemotional and advanced cognitive skills for employers is confirmed by the frequent use of these skills in employees' daily work. Virtually all workers at all skills levels are expected to be able to work on a team (figure 3.6). Many workers—especially professionals, technicians, and managers—are also expected to innovate and solve nonroutine problems. Basic cognitive skills are also intensively used in high-skilled occupations: the majority of

Figure 3.5 Ranking of Big Five Personality Traits by Ukrainian Firms in Four Key Sectors

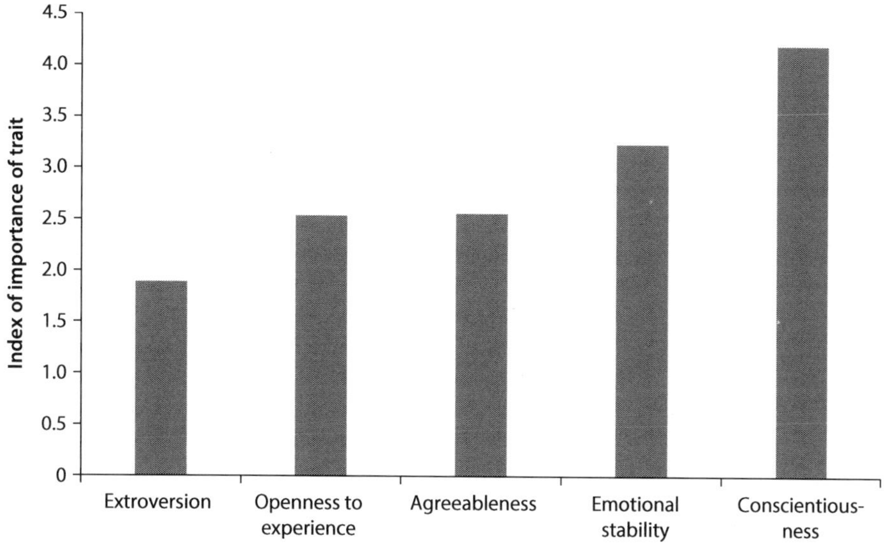

Source: Ukraine STEP Employer Survey 2014.
Note: The four sectors are agriculture, food processing, renewable energy, and information technology. Index is on 1–5 scale on which 5 is the most important trait for a given occupation, 4 is second most important, 3 is third most important, 2 is fourth most important, and 1 is fifth most important. The Big Five Personality Traits is a widely used taxonomy of personality traits (John and Srivastava 1999).

Table 3.4 Skills Requirements Cited Frequently in HeadHunter Job Postings in Ukraine

Type of skill	Specific requirements
Advanced cognitive	Communication, learning, time management, analytical skills, foreign languages, multitasking, critical thinking, problem solving, decision making
Socioemotional	Responsibility, stress resistance, self-management, goal orientation, teamwork, negotiation, organization, professionalism, teamwork, cooperation (agreeableness), accuracy (attention to detail), leadership, and perseverance
Technical	Sales skills, knowledge of markets and products, analytical methods, proficiency in field-specific software, knowledge of legislations, web programming, design, basic computer tools

Source: Job vacancies on HeadHunter online portal, March 2015.

firms' high-skilled employees regularly read, use math concepts, and write. Job vacancies on HeadHunter in March 2015 reveal employers seek a combination of advanced cognitive, socioemotional, and technical skill sets (Box 3.3). Advanced cognitive skills include good oral and written communication skills, the ability to learn, time management skills, and analytical and thinking skills (see table 3.4). Socioemotional skills include stress management (the equivalent of emotional stability), self-management, teamwork, professionalism and responsibility, and organization. These advanced cognitive and socioemotional skills are roughly similar to the ones identified in the four-sector firm survey. Frequently cited technical skills range from handling basic computer tools to

Figure 3.6 Skills Used by Employees in Four Key Sectors in Ukraine

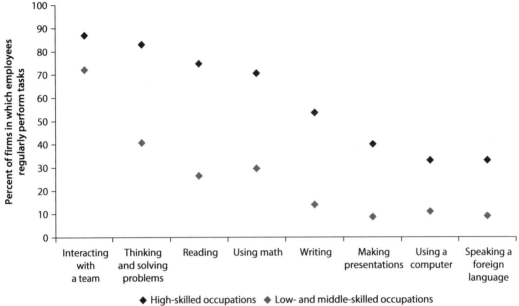

Source: Ukraine STEP Employer Survey 2014.
Note: The four sectors are agriculture, food processing, renewable energy, and information technology.

Box 3.3 Description of Data Set of Job Vacancies from Ukrainian Online Portals, 2015

A data set of vacancies in key employment portals in Ukraine was created for this study to provide information on demand for skills and other job requirements outside the four sectors studied. The data come from two portals, the public sector portal (trud.gov.ua) and a private sector portal (HeadHunter [hh.ua]), and was collected online in March 2015.

The public sector portal is operated by the State Employment Service (SES). All firms in Ukraine are required to register job vacancies with the SES and use the portal during recruitment. Many firms do not do so, however, preferring other recruitment methods, including private sector services (Kupets 2010). One reason employers often opt not to list their job vacancies with the SES is that job seekers who use public employment centers typically have low-level skills. Many firms do not hire workers registered as unemployed in the SES or use the SES's training services. The numbers and types of job vacancies posted on trud.gov.ua are therefore not representative. Gaining a meaningful sense of job vacancies therefore required data from a second source.

HeadHunter posts vacancies in 28 industries. It includes more information about the skills and occupational content of the job vacancies than the public sector portal does. Indeed, 70 percent of vacancies on HeadHunter cite various socioemotional and cognitive skills,

box continued next page

Box 3.3 Description of Data Set of Job Vacancies from Ukrainian Online Portals, 2015 *(continued)*

53 percent cite job-specific technical skills, 36 percent cite specific computer skills, and 26 percent cite the need to speak a foreign language. In contrast, only about 9 percent of listings on the public sector portal cite job-specific skills, with 3 percent citing computer skills, and about 2 percent cite foreign language and socioemotional skills.

There is also a significant difference between the two portals with regard to the education level required for the job. Employers posting jobs on HeadHunter are not required to include information about formal education requirements. Only 54 percent of the HeadHunter vacancies cite an education requirement; 44 percent of vacancies required at least some higher education (see appendix D for details). The online job application form at trud.gov.ua displays required education level; only less than 1 percent of all retrieved vacancies have missing information about education requirement. Employers may opt not to list education information when they are not compelled to do so for a variety of reasons. One is that they recognize that having a diploma or degree is less important than the worker's actual skills and work experience. Another is concerns about credential inflation and the mismatch between education and jobs. Comparison of the structure of vacancies in the HeadHunter and SES data sets by required experience (appendix D) seems to support this hypothesis.

For each posting, the data set identifies tasks/responsibilities, level of education, field of studies, job-specific technical skills, computer skills, foreign languages, cognitive and socio-emotional skills, formal-informal employment, working conditions, social benefits, additional requirements, and compensation. Vacancies were coded using the International Standard Classification of Occupations (ISCO) three-digit code, based on occupation and industry. The data provide a snapshot of the number and types of jobs available via these two sources in March 2015.

The richness of information in the private sector portal yielded details about job requirements (except education). Appendix E presents profiles in 16 categories. Vacancies in these categories make up 93 percent of all vacancies in the sample of jobs analyzed and 89 percent of all vacancies.

---

knowledge of the law and proficiency in complex software and analytical methods.

Job Categories in Demand

By Sector

Data from the public job vacancy portal indicate that the largest number of vacancies is in agriculture (26 percent of all registered vacancies). It is followed by manufacturing (17 percent); wholesale and retail trade and repair of motor vehicles and motorcycles (11 percent); public administration and defense and compulsory social security (10 percent); transportation and storage (7 percent); and human health and social work activities (6 percent) (figure 3.7). These six

Figure 3.7 Job Vacancies Posted on Ukraine's Public Job Portal, by Sector, March 2014 and March 2015

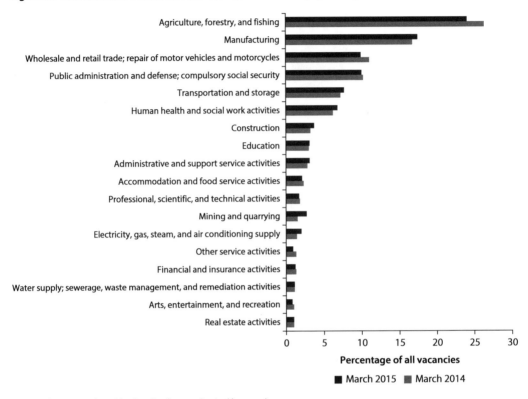

Source: Administrative data of the State Employment Service (dcz.gov.ua).

sectors accounted for more than three-quarters of all vacancies at the end of March 2015, as well as 12 months earlier.

By Occupation

Most vacancies on the public sector portal are in low- and medium-skilled occupation categories. Categories with large shares of vacancies include plant and machine operators and assemblers (25 percent), craft and related workers (15 percent), service workers and shop and market salespeople (13 percent), and unskilled occupations (13 percent) (figure 3.8). Low- to medium-skilled occupations (groups 4–9 of the ISCO classification) accounted for 73 percent of all vacancies. High-skilled occupation categories requiring tertiary education—legislators, senior officials, and managers and professionals—accounted for 18 percent of all vacancies.

The top 100 occupations (by number of available job vacancies at the end of March 2015) accounted for 68 percent of total vacancies on the public sector portal. Among them, 60 occupations (at the four- or five-digit level of disaggregation according to the ISCO classification) correspond to skill level 2 out of 4.

Figure 3.8 Job Vacancies Posted on Ukraine's Public Job Portal, by Occupation, March 2014 and March 2015

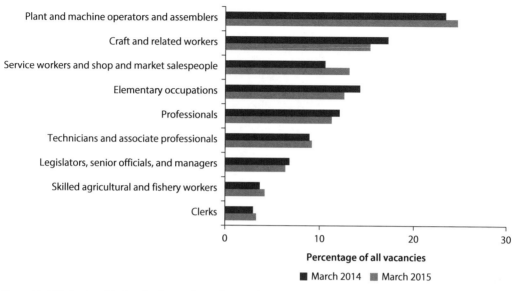

Source: Administrative data of the State Employment Service (dcz.gov.ua).

Figure 3.9 Occupations in Greatest Demand in Four Key Sectors in Ukraine

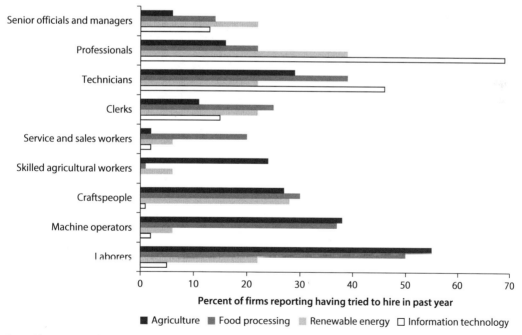

Source: Ukraine STEP Employer Survey 2014.

They account for 45 percent of all job vacancies (table 3.5). The next largest group, accounting for 12 percent of all vacancies, is skill level 1. It includes 12 elementary occupations. The top five—tractor driver, motorized farm equipment operator; car, taxi, and van driver; handpacker and other manufacturing laborer; and salesperson of food products—accounted for almost one-fourth of all registered vacancies (or 13,584 vacancies).

On HeadHunter, the largest shares of job vacancies are in the medium-high- and high-skilled categories. The professional areas most heavily represented are administration, marketing, advertising/public relations, IT, Internet, and telecommunications. The portal also includes many vacancies in manufacturing and sales. Some of the jobs posted were outside Ukraine.

The occupational categories for which firms from the four key sectors tried to hire new workers reveals heterogeneity across sectors. Almost 70 percent of IT firms tried to hire workers in the professional category, and more than 45 percent tried to hire technicians. In the renewable energy sector, firms sought to hire workers across all occupational categories. Nearly 40 percent of firms looked for professionals, and 20 percent sought technicians and managers. At the lower end of the skills spectrum, craftspeople and laborers were in demand. In the medium-skills category, clerks were in demand. In the agriculture sector, demand was concentrated in lower-skilled occupational categories (laborers, machine operators, craftspeople, and skilled agricultural workers); technicians were also in high demand. Demand in the food-processing sector was similar to demand in the agriculture sector (with the exception of farm workers, who are not employed in this sector, and service and sales workers, who are in high demand in this sector) (figure 3.9).

Table 3.5 Top 100 Occupations in Ukraine, Based on Number of Job Vacancies at End of March 2015

Skill level	ISCO one-digit occupation	Number of occupations	Percent of vacancies
4	• Legislators, senior officials, and managers	6	1.7
	• Professionals	12	4.8
3	• Technicians and associate professionals	10	5.0
2	• Clerks	5	1.9
	• Service workers and shop and market salespeople	18	11.9
	• Skilled agricultural and fishery workers	5	2.9
	• Craft and related workers	20	9.7
	• Plant and machine operators and assemblers	12	18.6
1	• Elementary occupations	12	11.8
All	Total	100	68.3

Source: Administrative data of the State Employment Service (dcz.gov.ua).
Note: These four ISCO skill levels have been defined in terms of the educational levels and categories of the International Standard Classification of Education (ISCED).

By Education and Work Experience

More than 40 percent of vacancies listed on the public sector portal required vocational secondary education, and almost one in four vacancies required complete secondary education (table 3.6). More than 28 percent of vacancies did not require education or training beyond a general secondary or vocational school diploma. About 27 percent of vacancies required the highest level of education (basic and compete higher education).

In eight sectors the majority of vacancies required basic or complete higher education (figure 3.10). At the other end of the spectrum, less than 1 percent of vacancies in transport and services for automobile transport, elementary occupations, and utilities (residential housing services) did so.

Not all vacancies specify requirements regarding the field of studies. Among the 6,795 that did, the top five fields were medicine (641 vacancies), business and management (570), accounting and auditing (467), law (437), and nursing (400).

By Region

More than 40 percent of job vacancies listed on the public job portal were in the four most dynamic regions of the country: Kyiv City and oblast (13 percent), Dnipropetrovsk oblast (8 percent), Kharkiv oblast (6 percent), and Odessa oblast (6 percent) (map 3.1). As a result of the ongoing conflict, the Luhansk oblast had the smallest number of vacancies.

The types of jobs posted reflect the main industries in different parts of Ukraine. Half of all vacancies in mining and quarrying are in the Dnipropetrovsk and Donetsk oblasts; 40 percent of vacancies in manufacturing are in the

Table 3.6 Education and Experience Requirements of Job Postings Listed on Ukraine's Public Sector Job Portal

Requirement	Number of postings	Percent of total
Education		
Not specified	172	0.7
Primary	200	0.9
Basic secondary (lower-secondary)	736	3.2
Complete secondary (upper-secondary)	5,647	24.0
Secondary vocational	9,412	40.1
Incomplete higher (tertiary, short-cycle)	980	4.2
Basic higher (tertiary, bachelor's degree)	1,507	6.4
Complete higher (tertiary, specialist's or master's degree)	4,819	20.5
Experience		
Not specified or no special requirements	10,924	46.5
None–3 months	99	0.4
1 year	2,007	8.6
2–4 years	6,385	27.2
5–9 years	4,039	17.2
10 years or more	19	0.1

Source: Data set of online job vacancies of the State Employment Service (trud.gov.ua), March 2015.

Skills for a Modern Ukraine • http://dx.doi.org/10.1596/978-1-4648-0890-6

Figure 3.10 Share of Job Postings on Ukraine's Public Job Portal Requiring Some Education or Training, by Sector, 2015

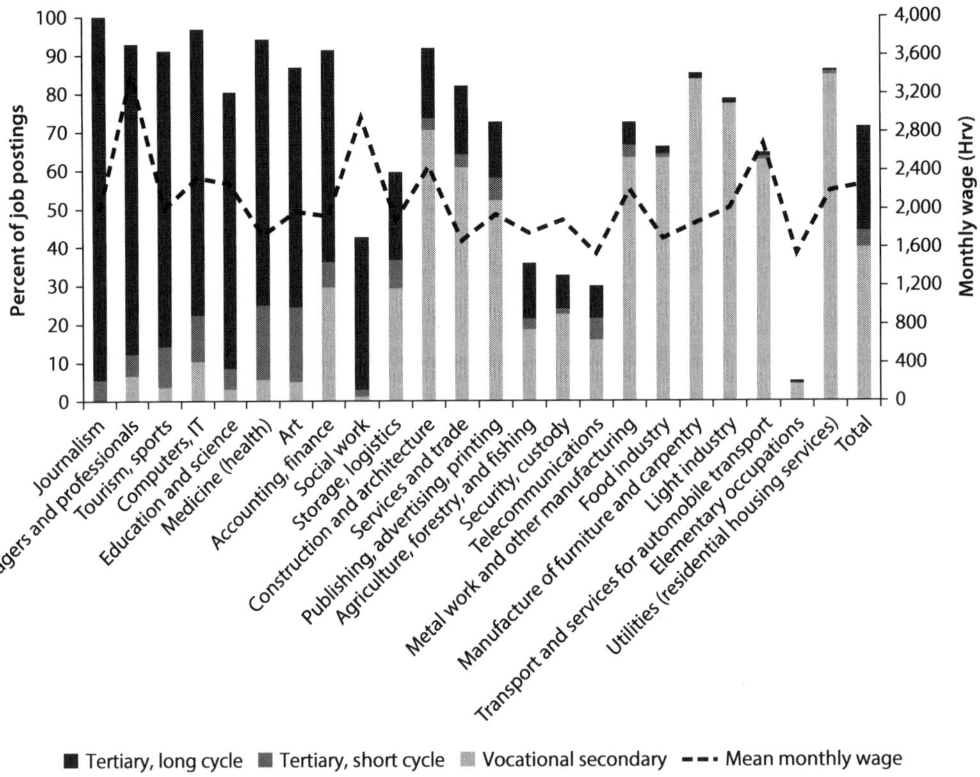

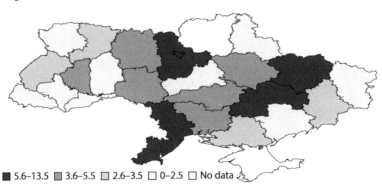

Source: Data set of online job vacancies of the State Employment Service (trud.gov.ua), March 2015.

Map 3.1 Percentage of Total Job Postings on Ukraine's Public Job Portal across Regions, 2015

■ 5.6–13.5 ■ 3.6–5.5 ■ 2.6–3.5 □ 0–2.5 □ No data

Source: Administrative data of the State Employment Service (dcz.gov.ua).

Dnipropetrovsk, Kharkiv, and Zhytomyr oblasts and Kyiv City; two-thirds of vacancies in finance and insurance are in Kyiv City; and 40 percent of vacancies in health and social work activities are in Dnipropetrovsk oblast and Kyiv City.

According to statistics about job vacancies published by the State Employment Service, there are also large differences in the importance of regions in the supply of vacancies within occupational groups. Kyiv City is the leading region in three broad occupational groups: clerks (28 percent of total); legislators, senior officials, and managers (22 percent); and technicians and associate professionals (24 percent). Odessa oblast leads in skilled agricultural and fishery workers, and Dnipropetrovsk oblast leads in plant and machine operators and assemblers and elementary occupations (figure 3.11).

Wage Patterns

Average wages offered in job postings are low. There is a weak correlation between the average wage offered in a sector and the share of postings requiring tertiary education (table 3.7). Although tertiary long-cycle education graduates earn higher wages on average, they are only modestly higher than those of vocational secondary education graduates. The average wage offered to college graduates is

Figure 3.11 Distribution of Job Postings on Ukraine's Public Job Portal, by Region and Skills Level, March 2015

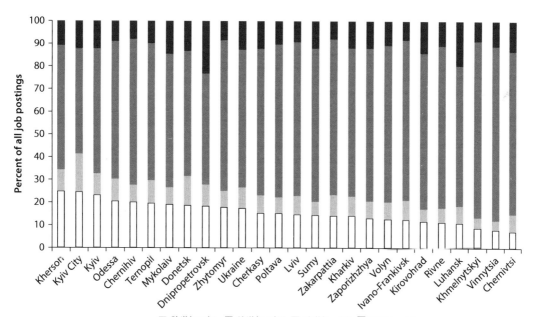

Source: Administrative data of the State Employment Service (dcz.gov.ua).
Note: These four International Standard Classification of Occupations (ISCO) skill levels have been defined in terms of the educational levels and categories of the International Standard Classification of Education (ISCED).

Skills for a Modern Ukraine • http://dx.doi.org/10.1596/978-1-4648-0890-6

Table 3.7 Monthly Wages Offered on Job Postings on Ukraine's Public Job Portal, by Required Education Level, March 2015

| | Monthly wages (UAH) | | | |
Education level required	Number of postings	Minimum	Maximum	Mean	Standard deviation
General secondary or lower	6,583	122	25,000	2,036	2,183
Vocational secondary	9,410	137	20,000	2,094	933
Tertiary, short cycle	980	221	20,000	1,858	1,103
Tertiary, long cycle	6,321	328	452,680	2,807	10,872
Not specified	162	406	10,800	1,758	1,054
Total	23,456	122	452,680	2,258	5,806

Source: Data set of online job vacancies of the State Employment Service (trud.gov.ua), March 2015.

Figure 3.12 Distribution of Job Postings on Ukraine's Public Job Portal, by Offered Wages and Occupational Group, December 2014

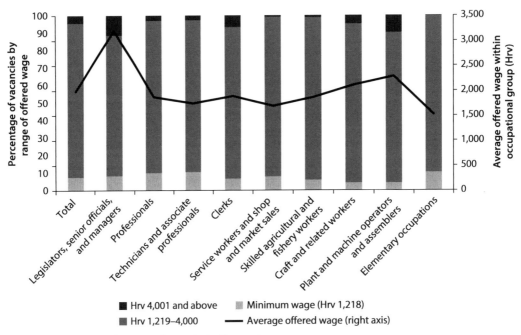

Source: Administrative data of the State Employment Service (dcz.gov.ua).

the lowest of all education groups. Average wages are higher for jobs requiring vocational secondary education (table 3.7).

The majority of vacancies listed on the public sector portal offered monthly wages below the average national level of Hrv 4,012. Only 4.3 percent of all postings; 9.6 percent of postings for plant and machine operators and assemblers; and 11.2 percent of postings for legislators, senior officials, and managers offered wages above Hrv 4,000. The average wage offered (about Hrv 2,000) was less than half the average wage in the economy in six of nine occupational groups (figure 3.12). The low wages offered explain why many job seekers, especially youth, men, and people living in the capital and other urban areas, choose not to register with the SES, instead using informal channels (family, friends), responding to job advertisements, and contacting employers directly for jobs (Kupets and Pidperygora 2012).

References

Cunningham, W., and P. Villaseñor. 2016. "Employer Voices, Employer Demands, and Implications for Public Skills Development Policy Connecting the Labor and Education Sectors." *World Bank Research Observer* 31 (1): 102–34.

Kupets, O. 2010. *Gender Mainstreaming at the Labour Market of Ukraine and Role of the Public Employment Service*. International Labour Office (ILO), Kyiv.

Kupets, O., and S. Pidperygora. 2012. "Characteristics of Unregistered Unemployment in Ukraine." (In Ukrainian.) *NaUKMA Scientific Proceedings, Economic Studies* 133: 89–93.

John, O. P., and S. Srivastava. 1999. "The Big Five Trait Taxonomy: History, Measurement and Theoretical Perspectives." In *Handbook of Personality: Theory and Research*, edited by L. A. Pervin and O. P. John. New York: Guilford Press.

OECD (Organisation for Economic Co-operation and Development). 2012. *Competitiveness and Private Sector Development: Ukraine 2011: Sector Competitiveness Strategy*. Paris: OECD Publishing.

Shevchuk, A. and D. Strebkov. 2012. "Freelancers in Russia: Remote Work Patterns and e-Markets." *Economic Sociology: The European Electronic Newsletter* 13 (2): 37–45.

World Bank. Forthcoming. *Broadband in Eastern Europe and Central Asia*. Regional Report of the World Bank Chief Economist's Office for Eastern Europe and Central Asia. Washington, DC: World Bank.

CHAPTER 4

Institutional Issues Holding Back the Creation of Jobs and Development of Skills

Institutional factors hinder skills development and the efficient allocation of labor. The formal education and training system is not providing students with the skills employers need, and it suffers from weak governance and an inefficient funding system. Little reliable information is available on current and emerging skills demands that would allow students, educators, and training providers to make good decisions or make their program offerings relevant to labor market conditions. Employers also see payroll taxes and social security contributions as major constraints to their operation and growth. Despite recent changes, the labor code and other labor market institutions do not facilitate an adaptable labor market or foster conditions that are conducive for the creation of more and better jobs.

Ukraine's Formal Education and Training System

Ukraine's education system suffers from low quality and weak governance. The majority of the labor force has tertiary education (the supply of university graduates having increased steadily since the 1990s), but the value of such education is low, making it difficult for employers to discern skills levels on the basis of educational credentials. In the case of older workers, many have obsolete formal education credentials and lack relevant skills for the new economic environment (Kupets 2015). This lack of signaling of formal education may explain why many workers hold occupations that require lower education levels than their diplomas (Kupets 2015). This lack of signaling may also explain why employers anecdotally report that they prefer to assess candidates through tests and interviews.

Most firms in the four sectors surveyed (agriculture, food processing, renewable energy, and information technology [IT]) report that the education system does not provide students with the skills employers need. About 70 percent of firms reported that graduates from the general education system and technical vocational education and training (TVET) system lacked practical skills and up-to-date knowledge (figure 4.1).[1]

Firms expect the formal education system to provide an adequately skilled workforce and to address skills mismatches through government intervention. They report heavy reliance on the formal education system to equip workers with the skills they need.

In the agriculture and food-processing sectors, firms want vocational education to address skills-related issues. In the IT sector, firms expect university curricula to change so that new graduates and people who return to school for retraining are equipped to function effectively in the workplace. They would like to partner with educational institutions to provide inputs into their curricula. In the renewable energy sector, which faces a shortage of workers rather than skills gaps, firms want the education system to encourage students to train for the sector. They also want the government to offer incentives for partnerships to develop renewable energy initiatives (figure 4.2).

The working-age population in Ukraine participates very little in skills training outside the formal education system. It is unclear from the data whether training opportunities are not readily available or whether people and firms have limited incentives to invest in training. Neighboring countries provide much more training (figure 4.3).

Figure 4.1 Ukrainian Firms' Views of Preparation of Students for the Workplace

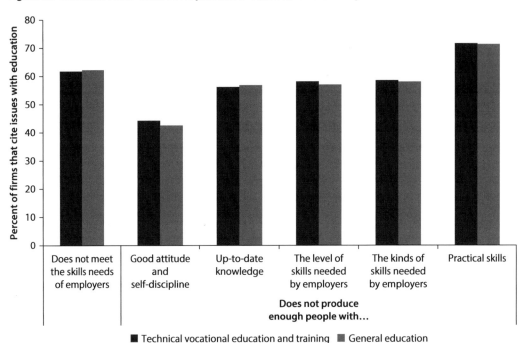

Source: Ukraine STEP Employer Survey 2014.
Note: Data are for firms in four sectors: agriculture, food processing, information technology, and renewable energy.

Figure 4.2 Areas in Which Ukrainian Firms Expect the Government to Improve Workforce Skills

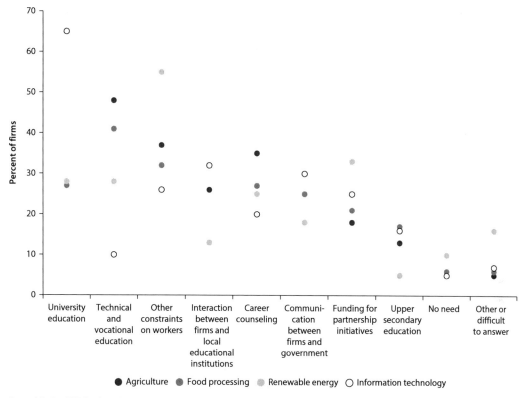

Source: Ukraine STEP Employer Survey 2014.
Note: Other constraints on workers include lack of housing, transport, and infrastructure that prevents firms from accessing a wider labor pool or prevents workers from fully utilizing their skills. Data are for firms in four sectors: agriculture, food processing, information technology, and renewable energy.

Less than a quarter of firms surveyed have regular contact with education or training institutions (figure 4.4). Although some training and education is demand-led, curricula formation remains a top-down process in which the private sector's engagement is limited. Less than 6 percent of firms surveyed reported providing feedback on education or training curricula (figure 4.5). Many of the firms that do provide feedback have partnerships with education and training institutions for recruitment.

Ideally, employers would work with educational institutions from the start (at the curricula-setting stage) rather than at the end (when graduates are ready to enter the labor market). Indeed, evidence shows that a good way to deliver up-to-date technical skills is for firms to team up with the private sector, especially at the vocational and college levels, where students are more likely to enter the labor market in specific sectors and occupations. One way to do so is to incentivize public-private partnerships that encourage the private sector to play a more active role in curricula modification. A good example is Chicago's college system, which was reformed to align its curricula and activities with the needs of employers (box 4.1).

Figure 4.3 Participation in Training in Ukraine and Neighboring Countries, by Labor Force Status

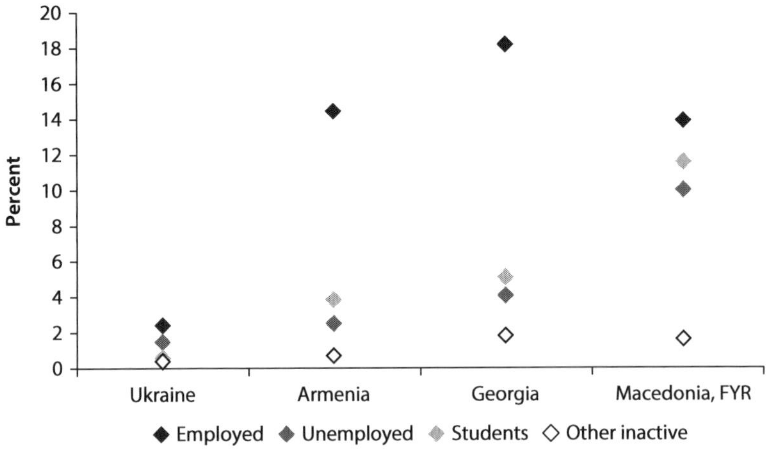

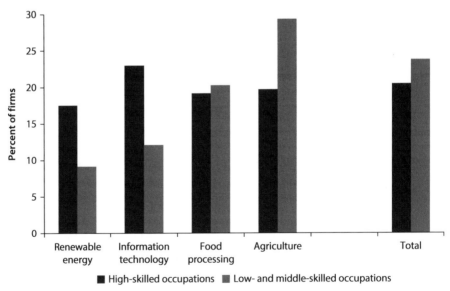

Source: Armenia, the former Yugoslav Republic of Macedonia, and Georgia: STEP Household Surveys 2013; Ukraine ULMS-STEP Household Survey 2012.
Note: Training includes courses, work-related training, and private skills training that lasted at least 5 days or 30 hours and were not part of the formal education system. Results are for urban areas only.

Figure 4.4 Share of Ukrainian Firms in Four Sectors That Maintain Regular Contacts with Educational and Training Institutions

Source: Ukraine STEP Employer Survey 2014.
Note: Data are for firms in four sectors: agriculture, food processing, information technology, and renewable energy.

Figure 4.5 Types of Cooperation by Ukrainian Firms That Report Regular Contacts with Education and Training Institutions

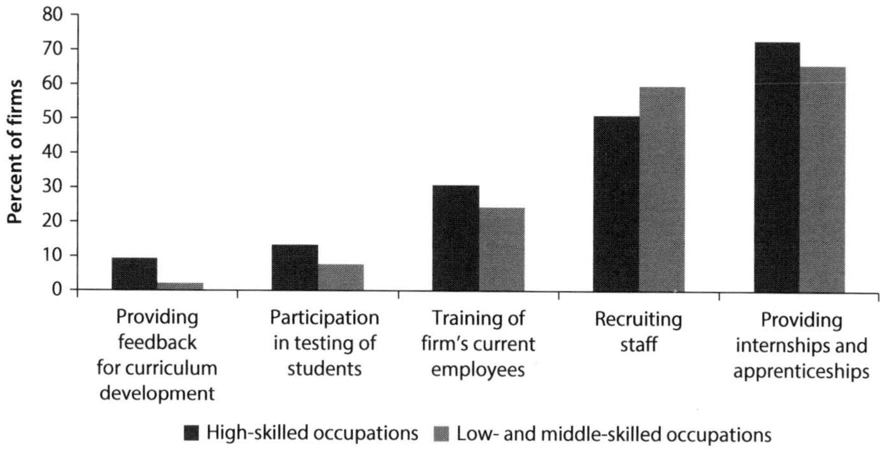

Source: Ukraine STEP Employer Survey 2014.
Note: Data are for firms in four sectors: agriculture, food processing, information technology, and renewable energy.

Box 4.1 Aligning the Curriculum with the Needs of Firms: How City College of Chicago Reinvented Itself

The City College of Chicago (CCC) is one of the largest community college systems in the United States, with more than 115,000 students in 2012. A 2010 review of its programming found several worrisome trends. It revealed that programming was not related to employers' needs, with courses that were either misaligned with or insufficient for the skills demands of employers. In particular, mismatches were identified in fields in which the number of well-paying jobs was growing.

After the review, the CCC launched a reinvention initiative called College to Careers, an ambitious campaign to reform how the system educates its students. One of the four core goals of the initiative was to ensure that more students received credentials of economic value.

CCC's review of the manufacturing sector illustrates how the process works. Review of its manufacturing programs found duplication and scattered instruction. Research also revealed that the manufacturing sector is the seventh-largest source of employment in the greater Chicago area. Review of the labor market revealed five career steps in the local manufacturing sector, from low-skilled employment (materials handler) to high-skilled employment (manager). Interviews with industry employers and experts showed that entry-level students were viewed as underprepared and that there was a demand for a more specialized core curriculum for entry-level employees. In response, CCC developed programming to fit these needs, in partnership with large employers, including Caterpillar and Kraft.

To meet the demands of the insurance sector, CCC partnered with companies, gathered job descriptions of entry-level positions, developed common skills requirements

box continues next page

Box 4.1 Aligning the Curriculum with the Needs of Firms: How City College of Chicago Reinvented Itself *(continued)*

based on those descriptions, and worked with faculty to identify important gaps in the curricula.

The initiative's partnerships have three primary goals: to revise curricula and the design of training facilities; deliver curricula through the use of teacher practitioners; and create a pipeline for internships, interviews, and training facilities.

As a result of College to Careers, occupational programming has been redesigned in six focus areas, six of CCC's seven campuses have been devoted to one of the six growth industries, and two state-of-the-art facilities have been constructed for health science and logistics training.

Figure 4.6 Nonlabor Market Issues That Constrain Firm Performance in Ukraine

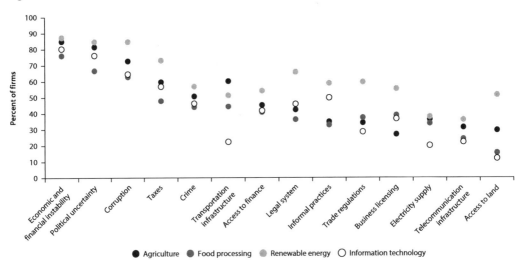

Source: Ukraine STEP Employer Survey 2014.

Beyond labor- and skill-related constraints, Employers in the four sectors also find that broader issues affect their ability to function and invest. Employers report that economic and financial uncertainty, political instability, excessive taxes, corruption, and crime are bigger problems for them than skills-related deficits (figure 4.6).

Building Transversal Skills through Training

There are common skills or competencies in the higher-skilled categories that employers expect the education system to teach workers. Occupational standards, available in high-income countries, show that there are common skills across occupational categories (within higher-, medium-, and lower-skilled occupations) that employers need for a worker to perform well. For instance, table 4.1 provides an example of competencies that all engineers are expected to be taught. Examples of advanced cognitive skills are physics, complex problem solving, and analytical skills. Among socioemotional skills, engineers are expected to be able to train others and to be active listeners. The specificity of technical skills listed for engineers varies depending on the type of field. However, they are all expected at least to be able to design, understand basic concepts of the production process, and monitor projects.

Among manual workers in the manufacturing sector, common competencies are also clearly expected. For instance, workers in the manufacturing sector are expected to have good coordination skills (table 4.2). Among technical skills, they must have knowledge of how to handle different types of equipment, the ability to be taught how to use and maintain equipment, a breadth of knowledge on how

Table 4.1 Common Competencies of Engineers (High-Skilled Occupations)

Advanced cognitive skills	Understanding of physics, strong communication and analytical skills, judgment and decision making, and complex problem solving	
Socioemotional skills	Active listening, active learning, customer and personal service, undertaking education and training of others	
Technical skills	Design	Knowledge of design techniques, tools and principles involved in production of precision technical plans, blueprints, drawings, and models
	Production and processing	Knowledge of raw materials, production processes, quality control, costs and other techniques for maximizing the manufacture and distribution of goods
	Monitoring	Keeping track of how well people and/or groups are doing in order to make improvements

Source: myskillsmyfuture.com.
Note: Based on U.S. occupation standards. Engineers include mechanical engineering technicians, agricultural technicians, and electrical engineer technicians, among others.

Table 4.2 Common Competencies of Manual Workers (Low- and Medium-Skilled Occupations)

Socioemotional skills	Coordination	Changing what is done based on other people's actions
Technical skills	Operation and control	Using equipment or systems
	Operation monitoring	Watching gauges, dials, or display screens to make sure a machine is working
	Dexterity	Ability to perform general manual tasks
	Equipment knowledge	Knowledge of machines and tools, including their designs, uses, repair, and maintenance

Source: myskillsmyfuture.com.
Note: Based on U.S. occupation standards. Manual workers include tractor drivers, manufacturing laborers, extraction workers, machine operators, and construction equipment operators, among others.

Skills for a Modern Ukraine · http://dx.doi.org/10.1596/978-1-4648-0890-6

to handle different parts of the equipment that manufacturing firms use (such as reading gauges and screen displays), and an ability to handle various systems. Fortunately, all of these competencies can be taught in vocational training systems as long as the equipment that is used is up-to-date by industry standard.

Ukraine's Workforce Development System

The government of Ukraine recognizes the importance of postsecondary education and training (hereafter referred to as the workforce development system [WfD]) for economic development. Both the National Program for Vocational Education and Training (VET) for 2011–15 and the National Strategy for Development of Education for 2012–21 set forth action plans for strengthening VET.[2]

Implementation of these plans and strategies has been constrained by the lack of financial resources and the ad hoc nature of coordination between government and nongovernment stakeholders. Funding for vocational training is not based on explicit criteria and specific performance indicators. Implementation of the National Qualification Framework, which seeks to align curricula with occupational standards, is a work in progress. Participation of the private sector in secondary and postsecondary VET is low. In contrast, a range of public and private enterprises provides training for adults. These programs need to be monitored and evaluated regularly.

Three overarching dimensions of Ukraine's WfD—strategic framework, system oversight, and service delivery—are assessed using a 1–4 scoring system. A score of 1 (latent) indicates that there is limited development and organization. A score of 2 (emerging) indicates the presence of a few good practices and increased levels of organization. A score of 3 (established) indicates a system that engages in good practices. A score of 4 (advanced) indicates a system that has adopted world standards of good practice. Ukraine's WfD system scores between 2 and 3, indicating an emerging system that has some good established features (figure 4.7).

Ukraine scores at the emerging level (2.2) with regard to strategic framework (figure 4.7), indicating that the system lacks clear direction for policy elaboration and implementation. Fragmentation of responsibility for WfD in the system makes it difficult for multiple agencies and actors to set a strategic vision, craft policy, and coordinate among themselves and with the business community. The biggest concern is the lack of engagement on the part of employers in setting curricula and monitoring outcomes. The low score in the demand-led dimension (1.4) indicates the need to reform the system in a way that allows employers to provide inputs into curricula setting and the functioning of the WfD system.

Legislation and agreements among stakeholders to promote coordination exist, and mandates of government stakeholders are clearly defined. The Constitution of Ukraine (1996), the Law on Education (1991), the Law on Vocational Education (1998), and other laws and regulations regulate education in Ukraine. Ukraine has made progress in developing new strategic documents, including the

Figure 4.7 Assessment of Ukraine's Workforce Development System

Source: World Bank SABER-WfD Data Collection Instrument 2013.
Note: The scores, ranging from 1 to 4, represent rating of the country's system development in the considered dimensions: 1 stands for latent (absence of good practice), 2 stands for emerging (instances of good practices), 3 stands for established (systemic good practices), and 4 stands for advanced (attainment of highest global standards). Ratings across dimensions are assessed by World Bank experts.

National Qualification Framework (approved in 2011), the National Strategy for Development of Education in Ukraine for 2012–21, and the State Targeted Program for VET Development for 2011–15. Nevertheless, implementation has been constrained by the underfinancing of programs and initiatives as well as the limited technical capacity of stakeholders involved.

The National Strategy for Development of Education in Ukraine for 2012–21 envisages the following tasks for the VET subsector:

• Developing occupational standards (and optimizing their number by integrating occupations)
• Optimizing the VET school network, in line with demographic, regional, and labor market realities, and expanding its autonomy
• Improving the mechanism of training workers by state order—the public funding of some postsecondary programs to train workers for the expected needs of the State or local administration. Make sure this system aligns with the needs of the economy.
• Providing professional development of teachers at VET schools

A clear commitment by the government to make meaningful improvements is evidenced by the large number of proposed (and approved) amendments to regulations that directly affect the functioning of the WfD. The Cabinet of Ministers has approved the National Qualification Framework (2011), the National Qualification Framework implementation action plan (by joint orders of the Ministry of Education with the Ministry of Social Policy), regulations on on-the-job training (2012), legal acts on recognition of nonformal vocational training (2014), and the procedure for further training of VET teachers (2014). It amended the procedure for providing on-the-job training and apprenticeship for VET students (2013) and employing VET graduates trained under the State Order (2010) and made changes to the regulations governing VET institutions (2013).

In 2014 the government adopted the Law on Higher Education, which significantly changed the structure of postsecondary qualifications. Ukraine's VET system has two levels: skilled worker (1–5 years of training) and junior specialist (2–3 years of training). Before approval of the 2014 law, the junior specialist qualification was also awarded by higher education institutions at the I and II levels of accreditation. The new law created a new junior bachelor's degree and a scientific Ph.D., and it eliminated four higher education accreditation levels. Other levels remain unchanged for now, although there are debates about transitioning from 11- to 12-year primary and secondary schooling.

Ukraine's legal framework requires further development. In particular, new laws on general and vocational education need to be introduced to bring the system in line with changes effected by the 2014 Law on Higher Education.

Donors and development partners play important roles in Ukraine's WfD system. Examples of their involvement include the following:

- The European Union's twinning project Modernization of Legislative Standards and Principles of Education and Training in Line with the European Union Policy on Lifelong Learning
- The EU-funded project Effective Governance of Labour Migration and Its Skill Dimensions
- The European Training Foundation (ETF) project Improving the VET System through Skills Anticipation and Adjustment, Social Partnership and Better Use of Resources (2011–2013) in Dnipropetrovsk oblast
- The Canadian International Development Agency (CIDA) project Skills for Employment, implemented in 2012–16 in Kyiv, Lviv, and Ivano-Frankivsk with a view to improving the relevance and training of graduates

The coordination between various stakeholders is challenging in most countries and Ukraine is no exception. The WfD relies on the participation of different government agencies (including the Ministry of Education and Science, the Ministry of Social Policy, the Ministry of Economic Development and Trade, and the State Employment Service) and nongovernment actors (including various employers associations, business unions, chambers of commerce, trade unions, and specialized nongovernmental organizations [NGOs]). Coordination and partnerships are often ad hoc. Policy dialogue is sporadic and deals more with sector-specific and technical issues than strategic priorities. Arrangements to monitor and review implementation remain less than optimal.

There have been some positive, albeit modest, steps to improvement. Assessments of national economic prospects and skills implications are occasionally conducted.

Employers participate in the National Qualification Framework, national VET standards and curriculum development, internships, and industrial training. Despite findings from assessments and participation of employers in key areas, however, industry and employers receive limited support from the government for skills upgrading, and few mechanisms are in place for employers to provide regular feedback. Although some WfD initiatives are demand-driven, policymaking remains a top-down process, and the private sector's engagement with broader WfD remains limited.

The second dimension assessed, system oversight, is an important function of the WfD authorities, because it measures whether there are systemic impediments to skills acquisition and mismatches between supply and demand. Three pertinent policy goals correspond to oversight mechanisms for influencing the choices of individuals, training providers, and employers: ensuring efficiency and equity in funding, ensuring relevant and reliable standards, and diversifying pathways for skills acquisition.

Ukraine received an overall rating of 2.2 (emerging level) on system oversight (see figure 4.7). The lowest score within this dimension is for efficiency and equity in funding (1.7). This rating reflects systemic weaknesses with respect to procedures for allocating and monitoring the effect of funding. Policy reforms in Ukraine often encounter implementation delays and difficulties because of lack of coordination and funding.

The system of funding needs reform to improve efficiency in allocations, ensure provision of textbooks, and upgrade obsolete infrastructure and equipment at vocational schools. It is important to shift from the current allocation mechanism for WfD, which is based on historical spending, to a system in which funding is tied to enrollment, performance, and effectiveness. Allocated funding should rely on formal processes that involve input from key stakeholders and timely annual reporting. Box 4.2 presents three examples of how funding is allocated to training programs delivered through initial vocational education and training (IVET), continuing vocational education and training (CVET), and training-related active labor market programs (ALMPs).

The relevance and reliability of quality standards is another central policy area in the WfD system. The National Qualification Framework was adopted in 2011 to support alignment of the education system with labor market needs. Employers have actively lobbied for the establishment of a national qualification authority to support the development of occupational standards and stimulate implementation of the National Qualification Framework. Such an authority has not been established. The Federation of Employers has taken the lead in setting up the Institute of Professional Qualifications to promote the establishment of sectoral skills councils for the development of occupational standards. This initiative provides an opportunity for public-private partnerships that can increase the institutionalization of the role of employers in shaping and managing the WfD system. Support is required to strengthen collaboration going forward. Support is critical because competency standards have been developed for only a small number of occupations (28 new-generation VET standards for occupations in

Box 4.2 Allocation of Funding to Training Programs in Ukraine

Initial Vocational Education and Training (IVET)

Local budgets are the main source of funding for IVET, at both the secondary and postsecondary level, even though training providers are allowed to charge tuition. Routine budgeting procedures for WfD funding are in place, based on historical trends rather than performance of vocational schools. Student support is provided mostly through scholarships, which are transferred to training providers and then paid to students. Support—including free training and retraining, preferential admission, guaranteed employment, and housing—is provided to students from disadvantaged groups, including people with disabilities.

Continuing Vocational Education and Training (CVET)

CVET is sector-specific and determined by the agenda of each ministry and its training institutions. The Ministry of Education and Science, for example, is responsible for the continuing education of teachers. The program is publically funded is thus limited to the professional development of staff from publically provided services (education, health, public administration). Reporting on CVET is limited; no national report is produced by any national entity.

Training-Related Active Labor Market Programs (ALMPs)

In 2014 the State Employment Service (SES) provided professional training to 202,200 unemployed people, including 34,800 at its VET centers. Training covers almost 200 occupations in demand on the labor market. The SES reports regional rates of employment of graduates upon completion of relevant training programs.

To support the competitiveness of older workers, the SES provided education and training vouchers to 5,700 people 45 and older in 2014. The largest number of vouchers was issued for training programs in land management, computer systems and networks, and software development, and for occupations such as tractor driver, welder, and loader driver. SES career guidance services covered 3.6 million people, including 1.4 million unemployed people and 1.2 million students (1.1 million of them in secondary schools).

---

demand on the labor market were approved and put into effect in 2011). Much more work is needed to improve the alignment of what is taught and what is required in the labor market.

In the pathways policy category, which evaluates whether workers can acquire new skills and competencies as well as keep their skills up-to-date throughout their working lives, Ukraine scores at the emerging level (see figure 4.7). Although pathways and recognition of prior learning are stated priorities of the government, the system has not removed obstacles to lifelong learning or provided recognition of informally acquired skills. The certification process is standardized and applies to all types of training providers. The WfD system offers a varied set of vocationally-oriented programs. Graduates of professional schools at the secondary level can enroll in postsecondary programs at colleges and universities. Despite these opportunities, the public perception of secondary professional education is negative, with such education seen as a last resort for the weakest students.

The third dimension assessed is service delivery, which includes enabling diversity and excellence in training, fostering the relevance of public training programs, and enhancing evidence-based accountability for results. Ukraine scores 2.5 on this dimension, the lowest score in the policy area (see figure 4.7).

Ukraine scores 2.7 with regard to excellence, which captures the diversity of nonstate providers active in the training market (because demand for skills is impossible to predict, having a diversity of providers is a feature of strong WfD systems). Ukraine is home to a diversity of training providers, both public and private. Most private providers offer adult training services and issue certificates. Relatively few provide initial VET; many offer continuing VET. The process for approving and closing programs is cumbersome, dragging down efforts to foster diversity and excellence. The National Strategy for Development of Education in Ukraine for 2012–21 envisages expanding the autonomy of VET schools. It is important to balance increased autonomy with accountability arrangements and to foster competition among VET institutions to enhance the provision of good-quality services.

Public training institutions need information on current and emerging demand for skills in order to keep their program offerings relevant. Ukraine scores very low (2.3) in this policy area. Industry plays little role in curriculum design, and dialogue with training providers is weak. Less than a quarter of firms have regular contact with education and training institutions. In contrast, links between training providers and research institutions are institutionalized, and there are some examples of efficient collaboration. Employment criteria for administrative and teaching staff of VET schools are acceptable, but there are limited opportunities for professional development.

Systematic monitoring and evaluation of service delivery is important for both quality assurance and system improvement. Credible data are particularly important in Ukraine in light of the large variety of training providers, which makes it difficult for parents and students to make informed decisions. Lack of information leads to misconceptions about the status and role of VET in relation to academic higher education. Ukraine's rating of 2.5 for development of this policy goal is the average of its ratings for administrative data from training providers (3.0), survey and other data (2.0), and use of data to monitor and improve program and system performance (2.5).

Amendments, proposals, and initiatives and the growing number of partnerships with the private sector and donors indicate a clear effort to improve the WfD system and align it with well-managed WfD systems around the world. Going forward, it will be critical for the government to follow through in six key areas:

- Stronger strategic leadership to follow up on the agenda and ensure coordination of stakeholders
- A more effective institutional setup for implementation of the National Qualification Framework

- Regular evaluation of the impact and enhancement of training programs for all modes of delivery with regard to graduates' labor market outcomes
- The link of funding to enrollment in and performance and effectiveness of training programs
- Mechanisms that leverage public-private partnerships to guarantee the systematic quality assurance and relevance of training programs
- The fostering of competition among VET institutions to enhance the provision of good-quality educational services

Ukraine's Outdated and Rigid Labor Code

Some of the challenges related to having a skilled workforce stem from regulatory failures. Ukraine's labor code is outdated and its labor laws overly rigid by international standards. Ukraine still has a pretransition labor code in effect since 1971 with numerous amendments, especially in recent years). Ukrainian employers are constrained by limited flexibility in their human resource management decisions. For workers, the limited portability of social benefits hinders them from moving to areas where more jobs are available and their skills can be better rewarded.

Although employment protection legislation is stringent in Ukraine (Muravyev 2014), firms view it as the least significant obstacle to their operations and growth in all surveyed sectors except IT. It may be that lax enforcement allows employers to evade strict labor regulations, reducing its effect on firms.

High labor taxation and burdensome labor regulations encourage informality, with deleterious effects on the quality of the workforce. Informality has been on the rise in Ukraine since 2008, rising from 22 percent of employment in 2008 to 24 percent in 2013 and 25 percent in 2014 (figure 4.8). It is concentrated among men; rural residents; young people (15–24) and old people (60–70); and workers in agriculture, trade, and construction (Kupets 2011). The worst-affected group appears to be older men in urban areas.

Most firms in the surveyed sectors are affected by high payroll taxes, social security contributions, and wage constraints (high overall and minimum wage). High operating costs (including compensation) force employers to forgo spending on activities that are not viewed as essential to the production process. Firms that perceive workforce-related costs as high are less likely to invest in training and more likely to use informal workers.

Taxes on labor increased in 2014 and 2015. In August 2014 the government imposed a temporary military tax of 1.5 percent on personal income. The tax covers all compensation, including base salary, bonuses, leave allowances, and sick leave payments. The personal income tax rate for salaries exceeding 10 minimum salaries—the equivalent of Hrv 12,180 a month in 2014 and 2015—was also raised, from 17 percent to 20 percent. As a result, the tax wedge—the share of the difference between total labor costs and net wages (equal to all taxes and contributions paid from a worker's salary) in total labor costs—increased by at least 1 percentage point (table 4.3).[3] For a firm in the lowest occupational

Figure 4.8 Informal Employment in Ukraine, 2004–14

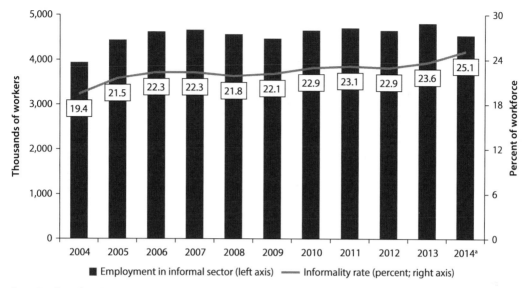

Source: Data from Ukraine's State Statistics Service.
Note: Figure refers to population 15–70.
a. Data for 2014 do not include Crimea or some territories of Donetsk and Luhansk oblasts.

hazard class (class 1)[4] paying average wages, the wedge increased from 40 percent to 42 percent; for a firm in the highest occupational hazard class (class 67), it rose from 45 percent to 46 percent. For firms that pay higher wages, which are subject to a higher marginal personal income tax rate, the tax wedge rose to as high as 47 percent.

High and increasing labor taxes during the economic crisis have likely affected job creation in the formal sector. Before the recent increases, labor taxes in Ukraine were at roughly the same level as many other countries in Eastern Europe and Central Asia (Rutkowski 2007; Arias and others 2014). Economists therefore concluded that the problem Ukrainian employers cited in enterprise surveys (and evidenced by the high incidence of underdeclared labor income) was not high tax rates per se but inefficiencies in the public expenditure system and pension provision.

In January 2015 the government introduced a measure that allows some companies to reduce their unified social contribution rate from 41.6% to 16.4%. The reduced rate can be used only by companies that meet stringent criteria, however: The monthly unified social contribution base per insured person must increase by at least 20 percent over the average monthly unified social contribution base in 2014, the average unified social contribution payment per insured person must not be less than the average payment in 2014, and the number of insured people must not exceed 200 percent of the average number of people insured in 2014. Few companies use the reduction. Firms suspect that the initiative is likely to be a temporary measure intended

Table 4.3 Tax Wedge on Labor in Ukraine, January 2014 and January 2015
(Hrv, except where otherwise indicated)

Item	January 2014				January 2015			
	Gross monthly wage of Hrv 3,167, occupational hazard class 1 (lowest)	Gross monthly wage of Hrv 3,167, occupational hazard class 67 (highest)	Gross monthly wage of Hrv 16,000, occupational hazard class 1	Gross monthly wage of Hrv 16,000, occupational hazard class 67	Gross monthly wage of Hrv 3,455, occupational hazard class 1	Gross monthly wage of Hrv 3,455, occupational hazard class 67	Gross monthly wage of Hrv 16,000, occupational hazard class 1	Gross monthly wage of Hrv 16,000, occupational hazard class 67
Unified social contribution rate for employers (percent)[a]	36.7	49.7	36.7	49.7	36.7	49.7	36.7	49.7
Unified social contribution payment	1,164	1,574	5,882	7,952	1,270	1,717	5,881	7,952
Total labor cost	4,331	4,741	21,882	23,952	4,725	5,172	21,881	23,952
Unified social contribution rate for employees (percent)[a]	3.6	3.6	3.6	3.6	3.6	3.6	3.6	3.6
Unified social contribution payment	114	114	576	576	124	124	576	576
Temporary military tax rate (percent)	0	0	0	0	1.5	1.5	1.5	1.5
Temporary military tax payment	0	0	0	0	52	52	240	240
Personal income tax rate (percent)[b]	15	15	15/17	15/17	15	15	15/20	15/20
Personal income tax payment	458	458	2,379	2,379	500	500	2,476	2,476
Net wage	2,595	2,595	13,046	13,046	2,779	2,779	12,708	12,708

table continues next page

Table 4.3 Tax Wedge on Labor in Ukraine, January 2014 and January 2015 *(continued)*
(Hrv, except where otherwise indicated)

Item	January 2014				January 2015			
	Gross monthly wage of Hrv 3,167, occupational hazard class 1 (lowest)	Gross monthly wage of Hrv 3,167, occupational hazard class 67 (highest)	Gross monthly wage of Hrv 16,000, occupational hazard class 1	Gross monthly wage of Hrv 16,000, occupational hazard class 67	Gross monthly wage of Hrv 3,455, occupational hazard class 1	Gross monthly wage of Hrv 3,455, occupational hazard class 67	Gross monthly wage of Hrv 16,000, occupational hazard class 1	Gross monthly wage of Hrv 16,000, occupational hazard class 67
Total taxes and social security contributions paid	1,736	2,146	8,836	10,907	1,946	2,393	9,173	11,244
Tax wedge (total taxes and social security contributions as percentage of total labor costs)	40.1	45.3	40.4	45.5	41.2	46.3	41.9	46.9
Share of social security contributions in tax wedge (percent)	73.6	78.7	73.1	78.2	71.7	77.0	70.4	75.9
Employer's share of social security contributions (percent)	91.1	93.3	91.1	93.3	91.1	93.3	91.1	93.3

Source: Ukrainian law.

Note: The Ukrainian law defines sixty seven classes of hazards for economic activities in the country according to the risk of injury or death at work. Before 2016, the level of social security contribution of employers was determined for each firm depending on its hazard class.

a. The maximum salary subject to the unified social contribution is equal to 17 times the minimum level (Hrv 20,706). The unified social contribution covers four types of insurance: pension insurance (88.3 percent), unemployment insurance (3.2 pe cent), temporary disability insurance (4.7 percent), and industrial accident and occupational disease insurance (3.9 percent).

b. A higher tax rate (17 percent in 2014 and 20 percent in 2015) applies to incomes that exceed 10 minimum salaries (Hrv 12,180).

to uncover underdeclared wages ("envelope payments"). For this reason, many firms are unwilling to apply for the new program. Preliminary estimates show that the tax cut could work only under certain conditions (Gorodnichenko 2015).

The new law on public employment came into effect in 2013. It imposes quotas on firms to hire special groups. Firms receive subsidies for employing certain categories of employees, including pre-retired people (men 50–60 and women 45–55), "young specialists" (people employed for the first time during the first six months after graduation), the unemployed, the disabled, and single parents. For companies with 20 workers or more the previous year, 5 percent of new hires must be from these groups.

Amendments were introduced to regulate paid internships and limit discrimination on the basis of age and gender. The law introduced financial incentives for employers to hire by replacing wage subsidies provided before 2013 with a rebate of 50 percent of the social tax for every new hire in a newly created workplace if the employee's monthly salary is more than three times the minimum wage; 100 percent for every unemployed subsidized person hired by the company and kept on for more than two years; and 100 percent for every unemployed person hired by the company and kept on for more than two years in priority economic sectors approved by the government (such as agriculture, food processing, energy, water supply, automotive, and telecommunications).

A new legal framework for outsourcing was also introduced. The law requires all companies engaged in employment-related services in and outside of Ukraine to obtain permits and licenses.

Amendments introduced in 2014 increased the liability of employers who fail to formalize employment or pay salaries, delay paying salaries or making other payments, or ignore minimum state guarantees on remuneration. The new law prohibits employers from hiring without issuing an internal order on employment and requires employers to notify the authority in charge of administering the unified social contribution of the hiring of any employee. If an individual works without entering into an employment agreement or works full-time while being formally employed as a part-time worker, the law enables the courts to deliver judgments on the formalization of the individual's employment and the period of such employment. The law nullifies employers' obligations to register employment agreements in the local office of the Public Employment Service of Ukraine.

Several important amendments were approved in 2014–15 to facilitate the mobilization of workers into the military without losing their jobs. The law stipulates that employees called up for military service during mobilization for a special period shall receive guarantees of preservation of their employment, job positions, and average income. It also establishes specific features of dismissal as a result of changes in the organization of production and labor in connection with activities during mobilization for a special period. They include guaranteed payment of pensions to retired military personnel called up for military service during mobilization and preservation of the state registration of business activities of individual entrepreneurs called up for military service during mobilization. Other guarantees related to mobilization are envisaged.

These amendments are needed given the current conflict, but they impose a significant burden on employers, especially small and medium-size employers. For this reason, only large and prosperous firms are able to comply with them.

Between 2010 and May 2015, 30 amendments were made to Ukraine's labor code. Few of them address structural issues that affect formal job creation and retention. The imposition of quotas and the protection of jobs for mobilized personnel increase the risks of hiring workers and raise the costs of labor. Some of these amendments make it more likely that firms will look for ways to prevent (formally) growing above certain thresholds. Many of these changes have had limited effect on the vast majority of workers and employers. Some of the amendments made in 2014–15 are likely to have a more meaningful effect on creating employment, at least in the near term. For instance, wage subsidization for broad sets of groups is likely to help the unemployed access work again. However, the fiscal costs of this policy will likely pose a threat to its viability in the medium term.

Notes

1. Employers reported similar issues with the TVET and general education systems; it is unclear whether they were unable to differentiate between the two or found both to be in equal need of improvement.

2. In 2012 Ukraine's government and social partners signed the National Tripartite Agreement on Employment and Jobs, which is in line with International Labour Organization's Global Jobs Pact.

3. There are some exceptions for special categories of employees (for example, disabled workers, pilots, members of parliament) and firms (public sector organizations, specialized enterprises for deaf or blind workers, air transport companies).

4. The Ukrainian law defines sixty seven classes of hazards for economic activities in the country according to the risk of injury or death at work. Before 2016, the level of social security contribution of employers was determined for each firm depending on its hazard class.

References

Arias, O. S., C. Sanchez-Paramo, M. E. Davalos, I. Santos, E. R. Tiongson, C. Gruen, N. de Andrade Falcao, G. Saiovici, and C. A. Cancho. 2014. *Back to Work: Growing with Jobs in Europe and Central Asia.* Washington, DC: World Bank.

Gorodnichenko, Y. 2015. "Ukraine Payroll Tax Cut: Can It Work?" VoxUkraine, Kyiv. http://voxukraine.org/2015/01/14/payroll-tax-cut-can-it-work/.

Kupets, O. 2011. "The Scope and Main Characteristics of Informal Employment in Ukraine." Technical Note, World Bank, Washington, DC.

———. 2015. "Education-Job Mismatch in Ukraine: Too Many People with Tertiary Education or Too Many Jobs for Low-Skilled?" *Journal of Comparative Economics* 44 (1): 125–47.

Muravyev, A. 2014. "Employment Protection Legislation in Transition and Emerging Markets." *IZA World of Labor.* http://wol.iza.org/articles/employment-protection-legislation-and -labor-market-outcomes-in-transition-and-emerging-market-economies.pdf.

Rutkowski, J. 2007. "Taxation of Labor." In *Fiscal Policy and Economic Growth: Lessons for Eastern Europe and Central Asia,* edited by C. Grey and A. Vourdakis. Washington, DC: World Bank.

World Bank. 2013. *What Matters in Workforce Development: A Framework and Tool for Analysis.* Washington, DC: World Bank.

CHAPTER 5

Identifying Core Skills for the Labor Market and Policy Recommendations

This chapter shows that workers need a mix of advanced cognitive, socioemotional, and technical skills to succeed in the labor market—a finding that is in line with evidence from around the world—and details which ones are most demanded in Ukraine. The same skills are highly valued across sectors and types of occupations. The chapter then describes the critical periods and actors influencing skills development across the life cycle and ends in presenting a range of policies to enhance the development and use of skills.

Key Skills for Labor Market Success in Ukraine

Identification of the skills most valued in the Ukrainian labor market is based on three methodologies and sources of original data. A household skills survey of urban areas sheds light on the relationship between measures of individuals' cognitive and socioemotional skills and labor market outcomes. A firm skills survey of four sectors (agriculture, food processing, renewable energy, and information technology) and a job vacancy data set reveal the specific skills employers value.

Comparison of insights from the three sources is not always straightforward, for several reasons:

- The nine skills included in the household survey and the 14 skills included in the employer survey are not identical and are measured differently. For example, the household survey does not directly measure technical skills, whereas the firm survey asks employers to rate how important technical skills are to them.
- Skills are measured and classified at different levels of disaggregation. For example, conscientiousness (a personality trait captured in the household survey)

includes many facets (such as organization, responsibility, and diligence) that are not captured as such in the firm survey or job vacancies.

• Coverage of all three data sources is not representative of Ukraine as a whole. The household survey covers only the urban population, the employer survey covers only four key sectors, and the job vacancy data set covers predominantly medium- and high-skilled occupations.

Different terminologies and levels of observation make it difficult to directly compare findings across surveys. For example, the household survey measures socioemotional skills at a broad personality trait level that includes many facets (for example, conscientiousness). The firm survey asked employers to rate the importance of socioemotional skills at a more specific behavioral level (for example, self-control and ethics, which are facets of conscientiousness).

Behaviors and attitudes cited in the employer survey correspond to facets of broader personality traits, such as those of the Big Five classification (see box 1.1). They can be mapped to other skills taxonomies to help operationalize concepts into interventions (table 5.1). For example, stress and perseverance, which correspond to the personality traits of conscientiousness and emotional stability, can be classified under the term *resilience*, defined as the ability to bounce back from adversity and thrive in the context of risk (Guerra, Modecki, and Cunningham 2014).

A core set of common advanced cognitive, socioemotional, and technical skills emerges from the individual and firm data (table 5.2). Although basic cognitive skills such as reading proficiency show little association with labor market outcomes (presumably because almost all workers in Ukraine have these skills), advanced cognitive skills—skills that allow workers to analyze and solve problems, manage their time, gain new knowledge, learn new methods, and communicate effectively—are in high demand. Employers look for workers who not only think well but also demonstrate socioemotional skills that help them manage their emotions and behaviors (such as control, resilience, ethics); set goals and be willing to learn (achievement motivation); and work with others (teamwork).

Table 5.1 Socioemotional Skills Demanded by Employers in Ukraine, according to Various Taxonomies

Skills demanded by Ukrainian firms	Equivalent in PRACTICE taxonomy of labor-market oriented skills	Associated Big Five personality traits
Professional behavior	Control and ethics	Conscientiousness
Self-management	Control	Conscientiousness
Stress resistance and perseverance	Resilience	Conscientiousness (grit), emotional stability
Goal orientation and motivation to learn	Achievement motivation	Conscientiousness (grit), openness to experience
Teamwork	Teamwork	Extroversion, agreeableness
Leadership	Initiative	Conscientiousness, openness to experience

Sources: Guerra, Modecki, and Cunningham 2014; Ukraine STEP Employer Survey 2014; HeadHunter job vacancy data set 2015.
Note: PRACTICE (an acronym for Problem solving, Resilience, Achievement motivation, Control, Teamwork, Initiative, Confidence, and Ethics) is a taxonomy of labor-market oriented skills elaborated by Guerra, Modecki, and Cunningham (2014).

Table 5.2 Core Cognitive, Socioemotional, and Technical Skills Identified as Most Valued in Ukraine

Type of skill	Specific skills
Cognitive	Problem solving, communication, creative and critical thinking, time management, learning, foreign language
Socioemotional	Resilience (stress resistance and perseverance), ethics, achievement motivation (goal orientation and motivation to learn), teamwork
Technical	Sales skills, knowledge of markets and products, analytical methods, proficiency in field-specific software, knowledge of legislations, web programming, design, basic computer tools, driving

Sources: ULMS-STEP Household Survey 2012; Ukraine STEP Employer Survey 2014; HeadHunter job vacancy data set 2015.

A core set of technical skills is harder to define, because they are often occupation- or job-specific and the only source of detailed technical skills (the job vacancy data set) tends to target higher-skilled occupations. Computing and programming skills are demanded in a range of occupations, along with knowledge of specific markets and laws, and sales skills.

Fostering Socioemotional Skills throughout the Life Cycle

Skills, in particular socioemotional, are by nature malleable and therefore can be fostered through interventions. Each learning context where skills are formed is influenced by direct inputs, environmental factors, and policy levers that can be used by decision makers to foster the development of a full spectrum of skills. Skills formation is a cumulative process. Interventions have to be implemented as an integrated set across the life cycle (see figure 1.2 in chapter 1). The benefits of investments depend on the accumulation of skills (Heckman and Mosso 2014; Kautz and others 2014). For example, children with solid foundations in cognitive and socioemotional skills developed in the first five years of life are better able to acquire advanced thinking and social problem-solving skills later on.

Interventions must be implemented when individuals are biologically and socially ready to acquire particular skills. Primary school-age childhood and adolescence are optimal (but not the only) periods—primary school, because that is when children first need to interact with others on their own (parents largely do it when the children are younger). In adolescence, more complex social interactions emerge due to neurobiological changes, larger influence of peer acceptance, and social changes, which provide opportunities to develop more complex patterns of social problem solving. The PRACTICE framework proposed by Guerra, Modecki, and Cunningham (2014) identifies the optimal age periods for developing socioemotional skills that matter for the labor market and explains how these skills relate to the broad-level facets of individuals measured in most studies (table 5.3). According to Guerra, Modecki, and Cunningham, the period between the ages of 6 and 11 years is optimal for all dimensions of socioemotional skills; younger and older ages are optimal for particular dimensions.

Table 5.3 Optimal Stages of Development for Labor-Market Oriented Socioemotional Skills (PRACTICE Taxonomy)

PRACTICE skill	Subskills (skills, attitudes, beliefs, behaviors)	Stage of development by age periods (and key actors)			
		Age 0–5 (parents)	Age 6–11 (parents, school)	Age 12–18 (school, peers)	Age 19–29 (school, family, workplace)
Problem solving	Social-information processing skills, decision making planning	Foundational	Optimal	Optimal	Reinforcement
Resilience	Stress resistance, perseverance, optimism, adaptability	Optimal	Optimal	Reinforcement	
Achievement motivation	Mastery orientation, sense of purpose, motivation to learn		Optimal	Reinforcement	
Control	Delay of gratification, impulse control, attentional focus, self-management	Optimal	Optimal	Optimal	Reinforcement
Teamwork	Empathy/Prosocial behavior, low aggression, communication skills, relationship skills	Optimal	Optimal	Reinforcement	
Initiative	Agency, internal locus of control, leadership	Optimal	Optimal	Optimal	Optimal
Confidence	Self-efficacy, self-esteem, positive identity	Foundational	Optimal	Optimal	Reinforcement
Ethics	Honesty, fairness orientation moral reasoning	Foundational	Optimal	Optimal	

Source: Guerra, Modecki, and Cunningham 2014.
Notes: "Foundational" refers to the initial skill-building process that will predominately occur in a following period. "Optimal" refers to periods of maximum sensitivity when it is easiest for individuals to acquire specific skills. "Reinforcement" means that intense practice is necessary to master the skill.

Resilience, for example, is best developed between birth and age 11; ethics is best developed between the ages of 6 and 18.

A variety of interventions at various ages and in various settings (home, school, work, centers) can foster socioemotional skills. Parenting, mentoring, and human interactions are the unifying themes of successful skills development strategies across the life cycle (Heckman and Mosso 2014; Kautz and others 2014). Early childhood interventions—such as interventions promoting parent-child interactions—have the greatest effect on long-term outcomes (Heckman 2006).[1] For school-age children, countries have implemented system-wide reforms to incorporate socioemotional skills in learning standards and curriculum, training not only children but also teachers and principals (Cunningham, Acosta, and Muller 2016). Many early- or middle-childhood programs also aim to foster cognitive skills. For adolescents, the most promising programs integrate aspects of work into traditional education or provide mentoring. Extracurricular and after-school programs using arts or sports to teach socioemotional skills are also valuable approaches. Socioemotional skills can also be included in job training programs in addition to technical training, as they have in Latin America (Ibarrarán and others 2015; Kugler and others 2015; Alzúa, Cruces, and Lopez 2016). For older individuals, skills are often acquired through on-the-job training

(Green, Ashton, and Felstead 2001). Many unknowns remain with regard to the right dose, sequencing, focus, long-term impact, quality, design of mechanisms, and incentives of such training.

Institutional Reforms That Could Foster the Formation and Use of Skills

Many challenges need to be addressed in the near term to increase productivity and help Ukraine emerge from a difficult chapter in its history. This section identifies the reforms that could be prioritized to achieve its goals.

Two overarching messages emerge from this study. The first is the importance of foundational skills, which are imparted in preschool, primary school, and lower-secondary school. These skills play a critical role in determining the quality of the workforce. Future workers need good foundational skills if they are to acquire a solid base of cognitive, socioemotional, and technical skills that will in turn help them gain new skills. They also need to continue to develop their skills to be adaptable to rapidly changing labor market needs.

The second message is the importance of institutional factors that facilitate (or hinder) how skilled and adaptable workers are and how quickly they are hired. These factors include links between education and employers, feedback mechanisms between education and training institutions and the labor market, an institutional environment that facilitates worker mobility, job-matching and training-intermediation services that ease the transition to jobs, and facilitation of entrepreneurship.

The section sets out four priorities and 12 corresponding actions the government could consider to move closer to meeting its goal of improving labor markets and making the economy more productive (table 5.4). The priorities are meant to improve the quality of worker skills, facilitate the creation of good jobs, and improve the effectiveness and efficiency of the institutional environment.

The analysis in this report highlights critical institutional and market failures that hinder the ability of the workforce to acquire the skills employers need. The most important failures include the following:

- The limited relevance of skills, which stems from the misalignment between the education and training system and labor market demands
- The limited use of information systems that could make the workforce system—workers, employers, and education and training institutions—more responsive and synergistic
- Insufficient use of opportunities for job-related skills training by employers
- An outdated regulatory environment that stifles job creation and investment in human and physical capital

Priority 1: Reform the Institutional Environment

- Reform labor regulations to reduce high labor costs, which disincentivize training and job creation. Many countries have reformed their labor codes in ways that support adaptation to changing labor market conditions and technology.

Table 5.4 Proposed Priorities and Actions for Improving Workforce Skills and Making the Ukrainian Economy More Productive

Priority	*Corresponding actions*
Reform the institutional environment	• Institutionalize a system that allows providers of education, training, and lifelong learning to identify the skills employers demand and integrate them into sector program curricula. • Reform labor regulations to reduce labor costs, which disincentivize training and job creation.
Reform education and training institutions	• Validate and align education and training curricula with sector employment needs and required industry credentials. • Improve the strategic orientation and oversight of the workforce development system. • Provide career awareness opportunities starting in secondary school, in partnership with local industry.
Create firm-level incentives to train	• Create systemic partnerships between employers and education and (formal and informal) training institutions. • Offer incentives for on-the-job and off-the-job training and opportunities for apprenticeships, internships, and fellowships, to provide early sector workplace experiences and entrepreneurship. • Evaluate and enhance social security contribution tax rebates to promote job creation and investment in worker skills.
Provide assistance to individuals	• Improve the effectiveness of public employment and training services to facilitate access to jobs, lifelong learning, and skills upgrading opportunities for all workers and training for productive entrepreneurship. • Improve the functioning of employment and training assistance programs to help vulnerable populations (especially internally displaced people and the long-term unemployed) acquire skills relevant to the labor market and become economically active. • Provide financial incentives for skills upgrading and continuous training. • Ease constraints to accessing financing for productive entrepreneurship.

Two factors deter investment in labor: high nonremuneration-related labor costs (employee benefits and payroll taxes) and inflexible labor contract arrangements. Ukraine leads peer countries in Europe and Central Asia with regard to the tax wedge on labor, which is as high as 47 percent (see table 4.3, in chapter 4). This wedge has almost certainly reduced new employment opportunities and noncritical investments, such as worker training and production upgrading. A full assessment of labor costs in Ukraine is needed to determine where costs are excessive and deterring investment in labor. In particular, the government could reconsider the recently added temporary military tax on personal income and social security contribution rates.

Ukraine's labor code limits employer flexibility in contractual arrangements. Evidence from around the world shows that increased flexibility can help employers adapt to changing needs and broaden employment opportunities. A revised labor code should avoid the potential risks of increased flexibility (for example, increases in temporary contracts) by reducing the costs of and establishing clear incentives for permanent employment. Examples of actions the government could consider are easing recourse to temporary forms of employment, increasing the length and scope of term contracts, and allowing flexible working hours.

- Institutionalize a system that allows providers of education, training, and lifelong learning to identify the skills employers demand and integrate them into sector program curricula. A methodology of web scrapping of job vacancies tested in this study provides a basis for such an effort. It should be continuously updated, broadened to ensure sectoral and geographic representativeness, validated with stakeholders, and integrated into the relevant education and training curricula.

Priority 2: Reform Education and Training Institutions

- Validate and align education and training curricula with sector employment needs and required industry credentials. Misalignments between skills needs and supply should be tackled through a set of government actions on multiple fronts. Measures should include further diversifying learning pathways, improving program quality and relevance, and disseminating good results from well-performing schools and graduates' labor market outcomes through various outlets. The government could also strengthen the link between the education system and the labor market by improving the management of the workforce development system, modernizing curricula using industry input, creating skills standards that are aligned with local needs and international standards, facilitating workplace learning, advancing cooperation at all levels of the education system, building regional skills alliances, and creating career pathways.

   A unified set of quality occupational and skills standards could be created and updated regularly, with the active participation of employers, to ensure that standards keep up with firms' demands. A unified set of standards would not only address the proliferation of qualifications issued by various providers, it would also improve quality assurance by establishing a single national standard and regulating body. Financial support and technical assistance from local and international partners, donors, and the private sector could be sought to ensure implementation and integration of the new standards throughout the education and training system. International experience from countries that have undergone similar reforms (including Australia, Ireland, the Republic of Korea, Malaysia, and the United Kingdom) could be assessed. Standards could be fed through the system at the institutional level, monitored through a rating system, and enforced by an oversight unit to ensure homogeneity across the workforce development system. The governance body could regularly review the standards, using a variety of labor market indicators to ensure a fit with labor market needs.

- Improve the strategic orientation and oversight of the workforce development system. Beyond identifying the right skills, the government could formulate an integrated plan to improve education, training, and access to good-quality lifelong learning. Without a strategy that includes lifelong learning, some segments of the workforce risk becoming unemployable. The education and training system should be open to workers and allow them to continuously acquire knowledge and skills. Lifelong learning should be an integral part of any skills strategy Ukraine adopts; many workers will need to be retrained continuously as industry continues to evolve.

The government could establish a high-level leadership committee to craft the strategic plan and hone the vision for the workforce development system, align its policies with the country's socioeconomic goals, enhance the national dialogue, and encourage industry and the public authorities to engage in more sustained and better-structured advocacy for workforce development. Lack of coordination among stakeholders currently impedes progress. The committee could help improve coordination.

The government could also support the creation of a body that promotes the establishment of sectoral skills councils, coordinates and advises on the development of occupational standards, and provides quality assurance for sectoral standards. An objective of this body could be to modernize the approach to postsecondary training by establishing clear (measurable) goals and linking funding and accreditation to set goals.

Evaluation of training is inadequate. To facilitate reform, it will be critical to enhance evidence-based accountability for results in workforce development by evaluating the impact of new and existing training programs on labor market outcomes.

Ukraine could develop national skills assessments and participate in international assessments such as the Organisation for Economic Co-operation and Development's Programme for the International Assessment of Adult Competencies (PIAAC), which measures cognitive and technical skills of the working-age population (15–64).

- Provide career awareness opportunities starting in secondary school, in partnership with local industry. Career and labor market information could be made available to students and their families early in the decision-making process to prevent misalignments. Outreach efforts could include introduction to the national (or local) labor market information system; introduction of secondary school–specific programs; establishment of prevocational and pre-university industry ambassador programs; and industry awareness training for secondary school counselors, classroom speakers, tours of firms and plants, and shadowing opportunities for students.

Priority 3: Create Firm-Level Incentives to Train

- Create partnerships between employers and (formal and informal) education and training institutions. There are some good examples of partnerships with the private sector in Ukraine, but the level of partnership is too modest to produce national results. These efforts could be scaled up to include a broader set of industries, companies, and educational and training institutions. To meet demand from employers, the workforce development system could partner with organizations in industry, gather job descriptions of entry-level positions, develop common skills requirements from job descriptions, and have partners review curricula and work with faculty to identify gaps in the curricula and areas that are relevant. Ukraine's public employment services could partner with the private sector to improve curricula and the design of training facilities, share equipment, establish teacher-practitioner arrangements, and offer apprenticeships/internships. A system of feedback between employers and skills providers should be established.

- Offer incentives for on-the-job and off-the-job training, apprenticeships, internships, and fellowships, to provide early workplace experiences. The government could consider creating an employer training investment program that helps businesses train their employees. Such a program could target companies looking to expand, relocate, or avoid closure. Program participation could be contingent on firms' addressing productivity concerns (by setting clear job creation/retention goals, for example). Fund-matching mechanisms could be included to prevent abuse. With respect to off-the-job training, short-term work schemes could retrain workers for occupations in demand in their local labor market.

- Evaluate and enhance social security tax rebates to promote job creation and investment in worker skills. In 2013 the government implemented such rebates (see chapter 4 for details). Before investing more in this program, the government could evaluate it to assess its effectiveness and ability to respond in a conflict context and make necessary changes. To ensure that the program benefits low-wage and vulnerable workers, the government could consider introducing a targeting mechanism.

Priority 4: Provide Assistance to Individuals

- Improve the effectiveness of public employment and training services to facilitate access to jobs and opportunities for lifelong learning and skills upgrading for all workers. The government could create a data-based profiling system for registered beneficiaries to facilitate a path to (formal) employment through training programs, internships, and funding for entrepreneurship. Such a tool exists in various European countries and could easily be adapted to the Ukrainian context. It could also be used to link individuals who are unable to work to short-term and long-term social assistance and avoid duplication in the provision of services. It could also help integrate internally displaced people by registering them and providing them with labor and social services.

  To facilitate the job-search process, the government could consider enhancing the labor management information system or creating a workforce dashboard (an interactive tool designed to visualize data and patterns related to the supply and demand of workforce, education, and training opportunities). The labor market information system (LMIS) should contain up-to-date information on vacancies as well as the education and competencies required for specific occupations; wage information by sector, occupation, location, and personal characteristics; current and future labor market prospects; and other relevant information. The State Employment Service (SES) could enter into partnerships with private providers of employment and training. Such partnerships have yielded positive results in other countries, particularly in crisis periods.

To make training services more effective and better aligned with labor market needs, the SES needs to improve the content of its training courses by making better use of up-to-date labor market information and strengthening its relations with employers to reform its curricula and train its instructors. It could focus on providing better employment and training services for socially disadvantaged groups (including unemployed, youth, displaced people, and informal workers) to facilitate their rapid integration (or reintegration) into the formal labor market.

- Improve the functioning of employment and training assistance programs to help internally displaced people and the long-term unemployed obtain skills relevant to the labor market and stay economically active. Evidence from other countries suggests that public works and temporary work programs can be effective in helping vulnerable groups overcome short- and medium-term economic hardships as well as in promoting longer-term employment. Public works are typically financed and implemented by a national or regional government or donor. Private employers hire subsidized temporary workers from the public employment services. The goal of public works is to provide participants with livelihood support (income) while simultaneously improving public goods and increasing participants' labor market readiness. Subsidized temporary employment seeks to provide workers at risk of long-term unemployment with access to on-the-job training and work experience. Both types of programs can provide training beyond the skills acquired on the job, preparing participants for longer-term employment, self-employment, further education, or training.

- Provide financial incentives for skills upgrading and continuous training. Providing financial incentives to firms and individuals to upgrade their skills is very challenging given the pressure the government is under to reduce public spending. Some countries have found financing modalities that are cost-effective, however.

  It is critical to support all institutional reforms with adequate financing, including financing to individuals, especially vulnerable ones, so that they can benefit from a reformed education and training system.

- Ease constraints to accessing financing for productive entrepreneurship. Providing training and access to finance for entrepreneuship and improving the business environment could yield potentially large payoffs in private sector development, both in easing the entry of new firms and facilitating the exit of inefficient firms (Arias and others 2014). Public interventions to foster entrepreneurship could spur job creation and raise productivity. Helping new start-ups emerge could help sustain job creation. Young firms ("gazelles") represent 12 percent of firms in Ukraine but account for 73 percent of jobs (Arias and others 2014).

Currently, entrepreneurs, or self-employed in Ukraine are more likely to hold such occupation by necessity than by opportunity. Two broad categories of entrepreneurs can be distinguished: subsistence entrepreneurs (people who are self-employed out of necessity and often lack skills and entrepreneurial traits) and transformational or opportunity entrepreneurs (innovative and expansive people, who are likely to have entrepreneurial traits) (*self-employed* and *entrepreneur* are used interchangeably here) (Cho, Robalino, and Watson 2014). About 18 percent of workers in Ukraine are self-employed; most work in subsistence agriculture and petty trade (Kupets, Vakhitov, and Babenko 2012). Many are de facto employees hired as contractors for tax reasons. They account for the bulk of employment in the informal sector (World Bank 2009; Kupets, Vakhitov, and Babenko 2012).

There is evidence of a substantial latent entrepreneurship in Ukraine. Only 15 percent of the labor force or 10 percent of wage workers starts a business. But a much larger portion—about 40 percent of the labor force—aspires to do so (Arias and others 2014). Many of these "latent entrepreneurs" are highly educated and work in the private sector as directors or managers. They represent a large potential for job creation, innovation, and economic growth.

Note

1. In Jamaica, for example, an intervention provided psychosocial stimulation (teaching parents how to talk and play with children) to poor stunted toddlers. Twenty years later, their earnings were 25 percent higher than those of the control group—enough for them to catch up with the earnings of nonstunted peers living in poverty (Gertler and others 2014).

References

Alzúa, M. L., G. Cruces, and C. Lopez. 2016. "Long-Run Effects of Youth Training Programs: Experimental Evidence from Argentina." *Economic Inquiry*. Early View.

Arias, O. S., C. Sanchez-Paramo, M. E. Davalos, I. Santos, E. R. Tiongson, C. Gruen, N. de Andrade Falcao, G. Saiovici, and C. A. Cancho. 2014. *Back to Work: Growing with Jobs in Europe and Central Asia.* Washington, DC: World Bank.

Cho, Y., D. Robalino, and S. Watson. 2014. *Supporting Self-Employment and Small-Scale Entrepreneurship: Potential Programs to Improve Livelihoods for Vulnerable Workers.* Washington, DC: World Bank.

Cunningham, W., P. Acosta, N. Muller. 2016. *Minds and Behaviors at Work: Boosting Socioemotional Skills for Latin America's Workforce.* Directions in Development—Human Development. World Bank, Washington, DC.

Gertler, P., J. J. Heckman, R. Pinto, A. Zanolini, S. Walker, and S. Grantham-McGregor. 2014. "Labor Market Returns to an Early Childhood Stimulation Intervention in Jamaica." *Science* 344 (6187): 998–1001.

Green, F., D. Ashton, and A. Felstead. 2001. "Estimating the Determinants of Supply of Computing, Problem-Solving, Communication, Social, and Teamworking Skills." *Oxford Economic Papers* 53 (3): 406–33.

Guerra, N., K. Modecki, and W. Cunningham. 2014. "Social-Emotional Skills Development across the Life Span: PRACTICE." Policy Research Working Paper 7123, World Bank, Washington, DC.

Heckman, J. J. 2006. "Skill Formation and the Economics of Investing in Disadvantaged Children." *Science* 312 (5782): 1900–02.

Heckman, J. J., and S. Mosso. 2014. "The Economics of Human Development and Social Mobility." *Annual Review of Economics* 6: 689–733.

Ibarrarán, P., J. Kluve, L. Ripani, and D. Rosas. 2015. "Experimental Evidence on the Long-Term Impacts of a Youth Training Program." IZA Discussion Paper 9136.

Kautz, T., J. J. Heckman, R. Diris, B. T. Weel, and L. Borghans. 2014. "Fostering and Measuring Skills: Improving Cognitive and Non-Cognitive Skills to Promote Lifetime Success." OECD Education Working Paper 110, OECD Publishing, Paris.

Kugler, A., M. Kugler, J. Saavedra, and L. O. H. Prada. 2015. "Long-Term Direct and Spillover Effects of Job Training: Experimental Evidence from Colombia". *National Bureau of Economic Research Working Paper No. 21607*. Cambridge, MA.

Kupets, O., V. Vakhitov, and S. Babenko. 2012. "Ukraine Case Study: Jobs and Demographic Change." Background Paper for the 2013 World Development Report, World Bank, Washington, DC.

World Bank. 2009. *Ukraine: Labor Demand Study*. Washington, DC: World Bank.

Description of the 2012 Ukrainian Longitudinal Monitoring Survey–Skills toward Employment and Productivity (ULMS-STEP) Household Survey

The World Bank's Skills toward Employment and Productivity (STEP) measurement initiative is a multicountry study that seeks to measure the supply of and demand for skills in urban areas of low- and middle-income countries (World Bank 2014). STEP surveys include a household module and an employer module. STEP surveys have been implemented in 12 economies since 2012 (Armenia, Bolivia, Colombia, Georgia, Ghana, Kenya, the Lao People's Democratic Republic, the former Yugoslav Republic of Macedonia, Sri Lanka, Ukraine, Vietnam, and Yunnan Province [in China]). All surveys included the household module; a subset also included the employer module.

The 2012 ULMS-STEP Household Survey is the combination of the fourth wave of the Ukrainian Longitudinal Monitoring Survey (ULMS) and the World Bank's STEP Household Survey. The 2012 ULMS-STEP Household Survey is representative of urban areas. It is based on a sample of 2,389. The ULMS is a panel household survey of adults (15–72), representative of the Ukrainian population (Lehmann, Muravyev, and Zimmermann 2012). The first three waves of the ULMS were collected in 2003, 2004, and 2007.

The survey includes information on demographics; education; employment and compensation; and household wealth, size, and composition (figure A.1). Modules include retrospective questions on employment changes since 1986, residence changes, and preferences for political regimes (Lehmann, Muravyev, and Zimmermann 2012).

The survey also assesses the cognitive skills, socioemotional skills, and use of skills on and off the job of a randomly selected individual between the ages of 15 and 64 in each household. An Assessment of their reading proficiency

Figure A.1 Contents of the 2012 Ukrainian Longitudinal Monitoring Survey–Skills toward Employment and Productivity (ULMS-STEP) Household Survey

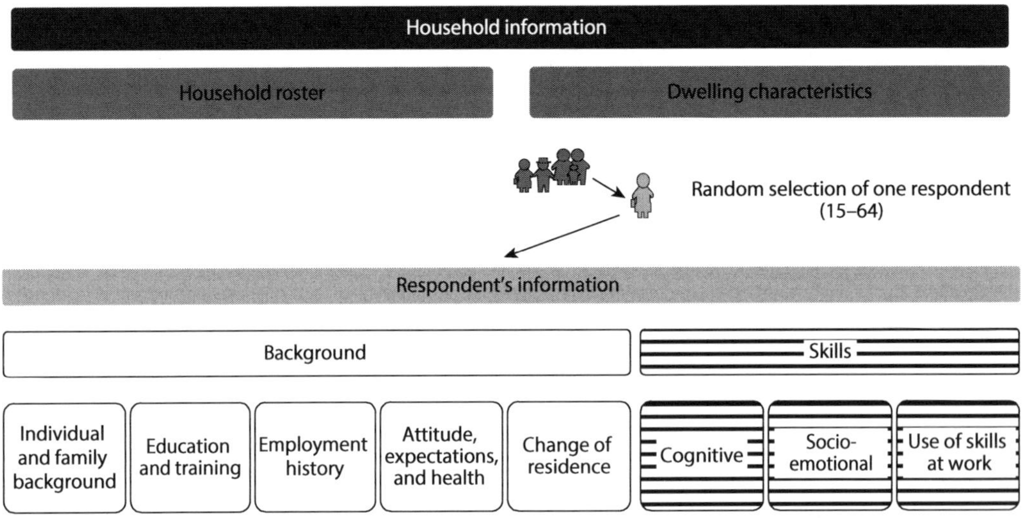

Source: Adapted from World Bank 2014.

assessment allows comparison of Ukraine with a dozen low- and middle-income countries (urban areas only) surveyed by STEP and more than 20 high-income countries covered by the Programme for the International Assessment of Adult Competencies (PIAAC) assessment of the Organisation for Economic Co-operation and Development (OECD). The survey also collects self-reported information on personality, behavior, and preferences (such as openness to experience, conscientiousness, extroversion, agreeableness, emotional stability, grit, decision making, and hostility attribution bias) and task-specific skills used on and off the job (table A.1). The skills covered in the survey include the following:

- *Cognitive skills.* The survey measures respondents' reading proficiency using a test developed by the Educational Testing Services (2014). Reading proficiency is defined as the ability to "understand, evaluate, use, and engage with written texts to participate in society, to achieve one's goals, and to develop one's knowledge and potential" (OECD 2012). It is a broader construct than the set of strategies used to decode written text. The assessment is intended to encompass the range of cognitive strategies (including decoding) adults must use to respond appropriately to a variety of texts in different formats and a range of situations and contexts (OECD 2013). Reading proficiency scores range from 0 to 500 and are grouped into six levels (table A.1).
- *Socioemotional skills.* The survey measures six personality traits (relatively enduring patterns of thinking, feeling, and conduct) and two behaviors and attitudes (how individuals manage intrapersonal and social situations).

Table A.1 Description of Reading Proficiency Levels

Level (score range)	Types of tasks completed successfully
Below 1 (0–175)	Tasks require respondent to read brief texts on familiar topics to locate a single piece of specific information. Knowledge of only basic vocabulary is required.
1 (176–225)	Tasks require respondent to read relatively short texts to locate a single piece of information that is similar to information given in the question. Knowledge and skill in recognizing basic vocabulary, evaluating the meaning of sentences, and reading of paragraph text is expected.
2 (226–275)	Tasks require respondent to make matches between the text and information and may require paraphrasing or the making of low-level inferences. Competing pieces of information may be present.
3 (276–325)	Texts are dense or lengthy (multiple pages). Understanding text and rhetorical structures becomes more central to successfully completing tasks. Many tasks require respondent to construct meaning across larger chunks of text or perform multistep operations to identify and formulate responses.
4 (326–375)	Tasks require respondent to perform multistep operations to integrate, interpret, or synthesize information from complex or lengthy texts. Many tasks require identifying and understanding one or more specific noncentral ideas in the text to interpret or evaluate subtle evidence claims or persuasive discourse relationships.
5 (376–500)	Tasks may require the respondent to search for and integrate information across multiple dense texts. Application of logical and conceptual models of ideas is required. Tasks often require respondent to be aware of subtle rhetorical cues and to make high-level inferences or use specialized background knowledge.

Sources: OECD 2013; World Bank 2014.

The socioemotional skills inventory is based on the Big Five model, a widely used taxonomy of broad personality traits that comprises openness to experience, conscientiousness, extroversion, agreeableness, and emotional stability (John and Srivastava 1999). The inventory also measures grit, a trait of perseverance and motivation for long-term goals (Duckworth and others 2007); hostile attribution bias, a tendency to interpret others' intents as hostile, which can foster antisocial and aggressive behavior (Dodge 2003); and the Melbourne Decision Making scale, which captures coping strategies for decisional conflict (Mann and others 1997). (See table A.2 for brief definitions of the socioemotional skills included in the survey and items used for the construction of scores of these skills.) The household survey includes 24 self-reported items designed by developmental and personality psychologists, which are mapped to one of the eight domains (socioemotional skills) mentioned above. The score for each socioemotional skill is based on the aggregation of these items (three on average). Response categories for each item range from 1 (almost never) to 4 (almost always).

- *Skills used on and off the job.* Self-reported items cover a mix of cognitive, (reading, writing, math, or problem solving); socioemotional (focused in this module on interpersonal skills like courtesy and counseling); and technical skills (focused on manual and physical tasks) (World Bank 2014). Items include the use of technology (such as the intensity of computer use and the complexity of software used), supervision of others, contacts with clients,

Table A.2 Overview of Skill Types and Domains Measured in the 2012 Ukrainian Longitudinal Monitoring Survey–Skills toward Employment and Productivity (ULMS-STEP) Household Survey

Type	Domain	Definition	Type of measure
Basic cognitive skills	Reading proficiency	The ability to understand, evaluate, use, and engage with written texts	Direct assessment (test)
Socioemotional skills (personality and behaviors)	Openness to experience	Enjoyment of learning and new ideas	Aggregation of set of questions designed by psychologists (self-reported)
	Conscientiousness	Tendency to be organized, responsible, and hardworking	
	Extraversion	Sociability and dominance in social situations	
	Agreeableness	Pro-social, cooperative orientation to others	
	Emotional stability	Tendency to feel negative emotions	
	Grit	Perseverance and passion for long-term goals	
	Decision making	How individuals approach decision situations (consideration of multiple options, of choice consequences)	
	Hostile attribution bias	Tendency to perceive hostile intents in others	
Use of a mix of cognitive, socioemotional, and technical skills	Use of technology, including computers	Frequency of use of computers; software used	Self-assessment of its use at work
	Supervision	Direction and checking others' work	
	Contact with clients	The extent of any contact with people other than coworkers, for example with customers, clients, students, or the public	
	Problem solving and learning	The frequency of learning new things at work and of tasks that require at least 30 minutes of thinking	
	Autonomy	Extent of the freedom to decide how to do one's work in one's own way, rather than following a fixed procedure or a supervisor's	
	Repetitiveness	Frequency of carrying out short, repetitive tasks	
	Physical and manual tasks	Extent of the physical demand of job, driving vehicle, repairing electronic equipment, operating heavy machinery	

Source: World Bank 2014.

problem solving and learning, autonomy and repetitiveness, and physical and manual tasks (Handel 2008).

References

Dodge, K. A. 2003. "Do Social Information Processing Patterns Mediate Aggressive Behavior?" In *Causes of Conduct Disorder and Juvenile Delinquency*, edited by B. B. Lahey, T. E. Moffitt, and A. Caspi. New York: Guilford Press.

Duckworth, A., C. Peterson, M. Matthews, and D. Kelly. 2007. "Grit: Perseverance and Passion for Long-Term Goals." *Journal of Personality and Social Psychology* 92 (6): 1087–101.

ETS (Educational Testing Services). 2014. *A Guide to Understanding the Literacy Assessment of the STEP Skills Measurement Survey.* Princeton, NJ: Educational Testing Services.

Handel, M. 2008. "Measuring Job Content: Skills, Technology, and Management Practices." Institute for Research on Poverty Discussion Paper 1357–08, University of Wisconsin, Madison WI.

John, O. P., and S. Srivastava.1999. "The Big Five Trait Taxonomy: History, Measurement and Theoretical Perspectives." In *Handbook of Personality: Theory and Research*, edited by L. A. Pervin and O. P. John. New York: Guilford Press.

Lehmann, H., A. Muravyev, and K. F. Zimmermann. 2012. "The Ukrainian Longitudinal Monitoring Survey: Towards a Better Understanding of Labor Markets in Transition." *IZA Journal of Labor and Development* 1 (9): 1–15.

Mann, L., P. Burnett, M. Radford, and S. Ford. 1997. "The Melbourne Decision Making Questionnaire: An Instrument for Measuring Patterns for Coping with Decisional Conflict." *Journal of Behavioral Decision Making* 10 (1): 1–19.

OECD (Organisation for Economic Co-operation and Development). 2012. *Literacy, Numeracy and Problem Solving in Technology-Rich Environments: Framework for the OECD Survey of Adult Skills.* Paris: OECD Publishing.

———. 2013. *Technical Report of the Survey of Adult Skills (PIAAC).* Paris: OECD Publishing.

World Bank. 2014. "STEP Skills Measurement Surveys: Innovative Tools for Assessing Skills." Social Protection and Labor Discussion Paper 1421, World Bank, Washington, DC.

Description of the 2014 Ukraine Skills toward Employment and Productivity (STEP) Employer Survey

The 2014 STEP Employer Survey gathers information on skills and labor issues from 702 firms (of a universe of 36,256) in four sectors (agriculture, food processing, renewable energy, and information technology) (table B.1). (See box 3.1 in chapter 3 for descriptions of the sectors.) Fieldwork was conducted between June and September 2014. The survey includes questions on skill requirements, hiring and compensation, training, and enterprise productivity (figure B.1). It uses the 1988 International Standard Classification of Occupations of the International Labour Organization (table B.2 and table B.3).

A large share of the firms surveyed were located in the Kyiv oblast, Kyiv City, and the three oblasts neighboring the Donbas region (see map B.1). No firm data were collected in the areas affected by the conflict or in Crimea.

Table B.1 Number of Firms Included in the Ukraine STEP Employer Survey, by Sector

Sector	Number of firms	Percent of all firms surveyed
Agriculture	260	37
Food processing	202	29
Renewable energy	40	6
Information technology	200	28
Total	702	100

Figure B.1 Contents of the Ukraine STEP Employer Survey

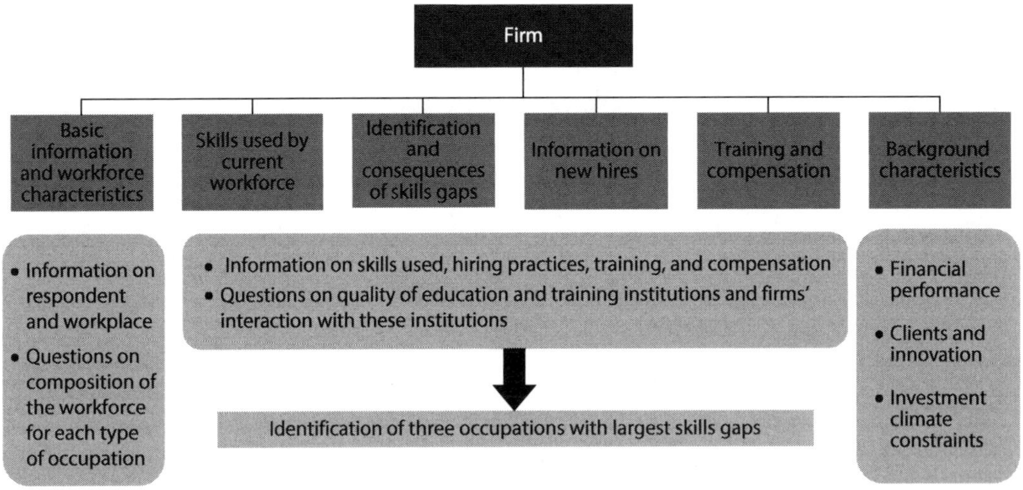

Source: Based on World Bank 2014.

Table B.2 Categories of Occupations Covered in the Ukraine STEP Employer Survey

Type	Typical education	Occupation category	Description of occupation categories
High-skilled workers	Tertiary	1. Senior officials and managers	Plan, direct, coordinate, and evaluate the overall activities of the firm or organization, and formulate and review their policies, laws, rules, and regulations.
		2. Professionals	Increase the existing stock of knowledge, apply scientific or artistic concepts and theories.
	Non tertiary secondary	3. Technicians	Perform mostly technical and related tasks connected with research and the application of scientific or artistic concepts and operational methods, and government or business regulations.
Low- and middle-skilled workers	Secondary education - general or technical - or vocational training	4. Clerks	Record, organize, store, compute and retrieve information, and perform a number of duties in connection with money-handling operations, travel arrangements, requests for information, and appointments.
		5. Service and sales workers	Provide personal and protective services related to travel, housekeeping, catering, personal care, or protection against fire and unlawful acts, or demonstrate and sell goods in wholesale or retail shops.
		6. Skilled agricultural workers	Grow and harvest field, gather wild fruits and plants, hunt animals, produce a variety of animal husbandry products, cultivate forests.

table continues next page

Table B.2 Categories of Occupations Covered in the Ukraine STEP Employer Survey *(continued)*

Type	Typical education	Occupation category	Description of occupation categories
		7. Craftspersons	Apply specific knowledge and skills in the fields to construct and maintain buildings, form metal, erect metal structures, set machine tools, or repair machinery, equipment, or tools, carry out printing work, produce or process foodstuffs, textiles, or wooden, metal, and other articles, including handicraft goods.
		8. Machine operators	Operate and monitor industrial and agricultural machinery and equipment on the spot or by remote control, drive and operate trains, motor vehicles, and mobile machinery and equipment, or assemble products from component parts according to strict specifications and procedures.
	None	9. Laborers	Perform simple and routine tasks which may require the use of hand-held tools and considerable physical effort.

Source: International Standard Classification of Occupations (ILO 1988).

Table B.3 Examples of Occupations Covered in the Ukraine STEP Employer Survey

Type	Occupation category	Examples
High-skilled workers	1. Senior officials and managers	Chief project or program manager, commercial manager, directors and chief executives
	2. Professionals	Computer systems designers, programmers, electrical engineers, veterinarians, lawyers
	3. Technicians	Computer assistants, agrotechnicians, accountants, bookkeepers, laboratory specialists
Low- and middle-skilled workers	4. Clerks	Transport clerks, office clerks, secretaries
	5. Service and sales workers	Guardians, server workers and shop and market sales workers
	6. Skilled agricultural workers	Animal producers, cattlemen
	7. Craftspersons	Bakers, repairmen, electronics mechanics and servicers, dairy-products workers
	8. Machine operators	Tractor and other vehicle drivers, food-processing machine operators
	9. Laborers	Manufacturing laborers, transport laborers and freight handlers, watchmen

Source: International Standard Classification of Occupations (ILO 1988).

Map B.1 Number of Firms Covered by the Ukraine STEP Employer Survey, by Oblast

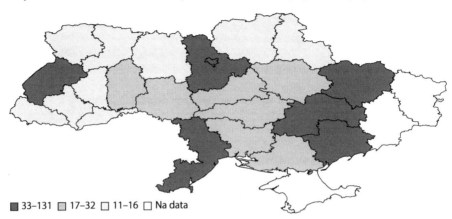

■ 33–131 ▦ 17–32 ☐ 11–16 ☐ Na data

Source: Ukraine STEP Employer Survey 2014.

References

International Labour Organization (ILO). 1988. *International Standard Classification of Occupations.* ILO. Geneva. www.ilo.org/public/english/bureau/stat/isco/isco88/index.htm

World Bank. 2014. "STEP Skills Measurement Surveys: Innovative Tools for Assessing Skills." Social Protection and Labor Discussion Paper 1421, World Bank, Washington, DC.

Methodology Used to Assess Workforce Development

The World Bank's SABER (Systems Approach for Better Education Results) is designed to help countries document and assess their workforce development (WfD) policies and institutions. It focuses on policies, institutions, and practices in three functional dimensions:

- *Strategic framework* refers to the process of advocacy, partnership, and coordination in relation to the objective of aligning WfD in critical areas to priorities for national development.
- *System oversight* refers to the arrangements governing funding, quality assurance, and learning pathways that shape the incentives and information signals affecting the choices of individuals, employers, training providers, and other stakeholders.
- *Service delivery* refers to the diversity, organization, and management of training provision—by both the public and private sectors—that deliver results on the ground by enabling individuals to acquire market- and job-relevant skills (for details on the SABER-WfD framework, see World Bank 2013).

Because these three dimensions create the operational environment in which both state and nonstate individuals, firms, and training providers make decisions about training, they affect skills development outcomes.

Each dimension is composed of three policy goals that correspond to important functional aspects of WfD systems (table C.1). Policy goals are further broken down into policy actions and topics that reveal more detail about the system.

Information for the analysis is gathered using a structured data collection instrument that is designed to collect facts rather than opinions about WfD policies and institutions. For each topic the instrument includes a set of multiple-choice questions, which are answered based on documentary evidence and interviews with knowledgeable informants. Each topic is scored on a four-point scale against standardized rubrics that reflect global good practices (figure C.1).

Table C.1 Functional Dimensions and Policy Goals in the SABER-WfD Framework

Strategic framework	1. Setting a strategic direction for WfD
	2. Prioritizing a demand-led approach to WfD
	3. Strengthening critical coordination
System oversight	4. Ensuring efficiency and equity in funding
	5. Ensuring relevant and reliable standards
	6. Diversifying pathways for skills acquisition
Service delivery	7. Enabling diversity and excellence in training provision
	8. Fostering relevance in public training programs
	9. Enhancing evidence-based accountability for results

Source: World Bank 2013.
Note: SABER-WfD is the World Bank's *Systems Approach for Better Education Results,* designed to help countries document and assess their workforce development system.

Figure C.1 SABER-WfD Scoring Rubrics

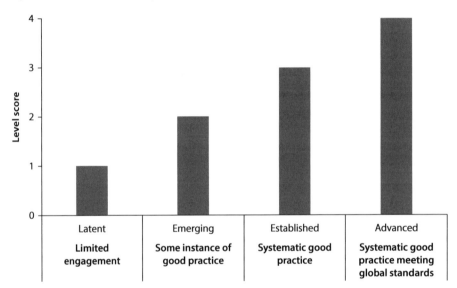

Source: World Bank 2013.
Note: SABER-WfD is the World Bank's *Systems Approach for Better Education Results,* designed to help countries document and assess their workforce development system.

Topic scores are averaged to produce policy goal scores, which are then aggregated into dimension scores. Relevant national counterparts, including the survey respondents themselves, validate the final results.

Strong systems of WfD have institutionalized processes and practices for reaching agreement on priorities, collaborating and coordinating, and generating routine feedback that sustains continuous innovation and improvement. In contrast, weak systems are characterized by fragmentation, duplication of effort, and limited learning from experience. The SABER-WfD assessment reveals the status of the WfD system and provides a basis for discussing how best to strengthen it.

Reference

World Bank. 2013. "What Matters in Workforce Development: A Framework and Tool for Analysis." *SABER Working Paper Series* 6, World Bank, Washington, DC.

APPENDIX D

Education and Work Experience Requirements in Job Vacancies

Table D.1 Vacancies Listed on HeadHunter Ukraine in March 2015

	Education required			Minimum experience required			
Professional area	No requirement listed	Higher education	Other level of education	None or up to 1 year	1 year	2–4 years	5+ years
1. Accounting, management accounting, corporate finance	26	74	0	5	23	52	20
2. Administrative personnel	61	36	3	49	33	14	5
3. Art, entertainment, media	81	14	5	19	52	19	10
4. Automotive business	75	25	0	13	25	44	19
5. Banking, investment, finance	27	66	7	24	45	28	3
6. Career starters, students	48	53	0	77	22	1	0
7. Construction, real estate	49	51	0	40	17	29	14
8. Consulting	43	50	7	43	14	29	14
9. Domestic work	88	13	0	38	38	13	13
10. Government, nongovernmental organizations	25	75	0	0	0	88	13
11. Human resources, training	34	63	3	12	20	48	20
12. Information technology, Internet, telecommunications	69	29	1	18	48	30	5
13. Installation and service	42	58	0	17	67	17	0

table continues next page

Table D.1 Vacancies Listed on HeadHunter Ukraine in March 2015 *(continued)*

	Education required			Minimum experience required			
Professional area	*No requirement listed*	*Higher education*	*Other level of education*	*None or up to 1 year*	*1 year*	*2–4 years*	*5+ years*
14. Insurance	46	54	0	13	54	26	8
15. Law	6	94	0	6	22	56	17
16. Maintenance and operations personnel	67	7	27	13	67	20	0
17. Management	26	74	1	3	7	62	28
18. Manufacturing	39	56	4	5	34	45	15
19. Marketing, advertising, public relations	70	30	1	59	16	23	1
20. Medicine, pharmaceuticals	25	73	2	9	45	39	7
21. Procurement	27	73	0	20	13	67	0
22. Mining and quarrying	18	82	0	0	27	18	55
23. Sales	49	49	26	26	41	26	7
24. Science, education	40	40	20	44	32	20	4
25. Security	64	36	0	23	64	14	0
26. Sports clubs, fitness clubs, beauty salons	68	13	19	21	40	40	0
27. Tourism, hotels, restaurants	68	29	4	18	32	43	7
28. Transport, logistics	59	41	0	24	27	38	12
Total	54	44	2	33	31	29	8

Job Requirements Included in HeadHunter Postings

This appendix describes the job requirements for 16 professional areas found in a sample of job postings retrieved from the Ukrainian online job portal HeadHunter in March-April 2015. A sample of 2,901 job vacancies was randomly drawn out of 7,486 web scraped job vacancies. 12 professional areas of which job vacancies represented less than 1 percent of the sample were excluded from the analysis, resulting in a final sample of 2,709 job vacancies. HeadHunter is the leader among job-sites for qualified personnel in Ukraine and may therefore not be representative of jobs overall. The authors of this study classified skills requirements are divided into five categories: technical skills, computer skills, foreign languages, cognitive skills, and socioemotional skills.

The 16 professional areas and their share of vacancies in the sample are the following:

Professional area	Number of postings	Percent of all postings
Accounting, management accounting, and corporate finance	129	4.8
Administrative personnel	518	19.1
Banking, investment, and finance	71	2.6
Construction and real estate	142	5.2
Human resources and training	37	1.4
Information technology, Internet, and telecommunications	59	2.2
Jobs for career starters and students	39	1.4
Maintenance and operations personnel	396	14.6
Management	146	5.4
Manufacturing	295	10.9

table continues next page

Professional area	Number of postings	Percent of all postings
Marketing, advertising, and public relations	547	20.2
Medicine and pharmaceuticals	58	2.1
Sales	153	5.6
Sports and beauty salons	54	2.0
Tourism, hotels, and restaurants	29	1.1
Transport and logistics	36	1.3
Total	2,709	100

Note: The following professional areas represented less than 1 percent of the sample and were excluded from it: Science and Education; Art, Entertainment, and Media; Security; Lawyers; Automotive Business; Consulting; Maintenance and Operations Personnel; Procurement; Installation and Service; Raw Materials; Domestic Staff.

Accounting, Management Accounting, and Corporate Finance

This professional area includes finance managers, accountants, auditors, and economists.

Education and experience. Three-quarters of postings required higher education (in accounting, auditing, finance, or economics); the rest did not cite education requirements. Three-quarters of postings required at least two years of experience.

Technical skills. Proficiency in tax accounting and financial and economic analysis; knowledge of primary accounting documents; knowledge of current legal framework (mainly on taxation but sometimes also on labor, foreign trade activities, and banking activities) and ability to apply it; and international standards of reporting. Some postings required certification, including Certified Accounting Practitioner (CAP), Certified International Professional Accountant (CIPA), Diploma in International Financial Reporting (DipIFR), Chartered Institute of Management Accountants (CIMA), and Chartered Financial Analyst (CFA).

Computer skills. MS Office, 1C, advanced computer skills, and online banking.

Foreign language. Only a quarter of postings required proficiency in a foreign language (mainly English).

Cognitive skills. Communication, time management, thinking, and data analysis skills.

Socioemotional skills. Responsibility, attentiveness, honesty, accuracy, self-management, and stress management.

Administrative Personnel

This professional area includes personal assistants of directors, office managers, and administrators; secretaries; receptionists; translators; computer operators; operators of call centers; and some couriers, cleaners, and drivers.

Operators of Call Centers and Data Entry Clerks

Education and experience. Few jobs cited education requirements. Some postings required at least incomplete higher education (secondary specialized). Eighty percent required no work experience.

Technical skills. Nearly 70 percent of postings did not cite technical skills. When technical skills are cited, postings mentions good diction and ability to operate office equipment

Computer skills. About half of postings required basic computer tools (mainly Word, Excel, and Internet, and e-mail).

Foreign language. Almost half of postings required proficiency in a foreign language, predominantly Russian.

Cognitive skills. Most postings required communication (oral and written, presentation), learning, time management, and thinking skills.

Socioemotional skills. Most postings required agreeableness, responsibility, proactiveness, attentiveness, and perseverance.

Office Managers, Administrators, and Secretaries

Education and experience. More than half of job postings did not cite educational requirements. Those that did usually required basic or completed higher education (long-cycle). Most postings required some work experience (usually one to four years).

Technical skills. Many postings required knowledge of business correspondence and etiquette and some knowledge of labor legislation and human resources. Many required the ability to operate office equipment and manage employees (at small companies office managers function as human resources managers).

Computer skills. Half of all postings required computer skills, mainly proficiency in MS Office (Word, Excel, Outlook, and PowerPoint) and the Internet; some also required knowledge of the accounting software 1C.

Foreign language. Many postings required proficiency in English, sometimes in Ukrainian and Russian (in writing or orally).

Cognitive skills. Most postings required (oral and written, presentation), learning, time management, and multitasking skills.

Socioemotional skills. Responsibility, attentiveness, organization, perseverance, self-management, goal orientation, orderliness, and stress management.

Banking, Investment, and Finance

This professional area included postings at various levels in the banking, investment, and finance sectors. More than 20 percent of all postings came from Privatbank, the largest private bank in Ukraine.

Education and experience. Seventy percent of postings required at least incomplete higher education (short-cycle, vocational). Most required complete higher education in economics or finance, with some postings looking for law, information technology, math, or management degrees. More than three-quarters of postings required at least one year of experience.

Technical skills. Most postings required sales skills; knowledge of the legal framework for banking activities, particularly central bank regulations on banking operations and nonperforming loans; knowledge of cash-management products,

Society for Worldwide Interbank Financial Telecommunication (SWIFT) standards, pay systems, and online banking.

Computer skills. Only a quarter of vacancies required some computer skills (mainly basic computer tools). Presumably such skills are taken for granted.

Foreign language. Less than 20 percent of postings required fluency in a foreign language. Only a few postings (mainly by international firms and their subsidiaries) required good command of English or Russian.

Cognitive skills. Most postings required communication (oral), learning, and time management skills.

Socioemotional skills. Most postings required goal orientation, responsibility, negotiation, stress management, and agreeableness.

Construction and Real Estate

This professional area includes professionals and associate professionals in construction and real estate agents.

Education and experience. More than half of postings required higher education (mainly complete, such as a specialist's or master's degree). Forty percent of postings (including all postings for real estate agents) did not require work experience.

Technical skills. Knowledge of regulatory framework in the construction sector, organization of construction works, norms of expenses of building materials, engineering and residential communications, regulatory documents, active sales, legislation regulating investment activity, evaluation of investment projects, and sales techniques.

Computer skills. About 60 percent of postings required some computer skills, with many requiring proficiency in special software for two- and three-dimensional modeling (such as ArchiCAD, AutoCAD, 3D Max and VRay, SketchUp, and Adobe Creative Suite).

Foreign language. No postings required fluency in English.

Cognitive skills. Most postings required communication and learning skills.

Socioemotional skills. Most postings required proactiveness, responsibility, goal orientation, and teamwork.

Human Resources and Training

This professional area includes human resource managers and specialists, recruitment specialists, and trainers.

Education and experience. Sixty-three percent of postings required higher education and 88 percent required at least one year of relevant work experience (20 percent of postings required at least five years).

Technical skills. Most postings required knowledge of labor legislation, recruiting assessment tools and tests, staff development and training, corporate culture, and current labor market situation.

Computer skills. Forty percent of postings required knowledge of basic computer tools (Word, Excel, and Internet), some required proficiency in the accounting software 1C or social networks (Vkontakte, Facebook, LinkedIn).

Foreign language. About a fifth of postings required some level of English. Some postings required other languages (French, Dutch, Turkish, Spanish, or Polish).

Cognitive skills. Most postings required communication, learning, management, and decision-making skills.

Socioemotional skills. Most postings required interpersonal skills, responsibility, goal orientation, leadership, and organization.

Information Technology, Internet, and Telecommunications

This professional area includes software developers, project managers, sales specialists, telecommunications professionals, database administrators, system administrators, testers, analysts, and related professionals. Firms in this sector seem to invest more in workforce development (English training, for example) than any other sector. They offer attractive working conditions, including flexible schedules and long-distance working arrangements.

Education and experience. Only 30 percent of postings cited educational requirements (mainly higher education in information technology, computer science, applied math, and engineering). More than 80 percent cited at least one year of experience.

Computer skills. Most postings required proficiency in special software and programming languages, such as C, C^{++}, C$^{\#}$, and. Net; PHP, Linux, MySQL, Apache, and Python; HTML, CSS, JavaScript, Twitter Bootstrap/Zurb Foundation, jQuery/Dojo, SASS/LESS, and Angular/Backbone/Knockout; Adobe Illustrator, Adobe Photoshop, Adobe InDesign, CorelDraw, and Dreamweaver; and Google Analytics, Yandex Metrics, Facebook, and VKontakte, among many others.

Foreign language. More than 40 percent of postings required fluency in a foreign language, most often English (at least intermediate proficiency and knowledge of technical vocabulary).

Cognitive skills. Most postings required communication (including presentation), learning, time management, and thinking skills.

Socioemotional skills. Most postings required responsability, teamwork, self-management, goal orientation, attention to detail, and stress management.

Jobs for Career Starters and Students

This professional area includes interns and entry-level jobs (assistants to professionals in marketing, banking, call centers, and sales).

Education and experience. Some level of higher education (including incomplete) was required in half of postings, likely to compensate for lack of experience, which only a quarter of postings required.

Technical skills. Most postings required background theoretical and practical knowledge rather than specific technical skills.

Computer skills. About a third of postings required some computer skills, mostly basic tools (MS Office, Internet, e-mail). Postings in programming, graphic design, and engineering required knowledge of special software.

Foreign language. More than 30 percent of postings required fluency in a foreign language (mostly English, sometimes Russian).

Cognitive skills. Most postings required communication time management, and learning skills.

Socioemotional skills. Most postings required responsibility, stress management, teamwork, organization, grit, and initiative.

Maintenance and Operations Personnel

This professional area includes machine operators, seamstresses, turners, and some other craftspersons and laborers.

Education and experience. Most postings did not include educational requirements. Most required at least one year of experience.

Technical skills. Depends on occupation; many postings did not include requirements linked to technical skills.

Computer skills. No special requirements in most cases.

Foreign language. No special requirements in most cases.

Cognitive skills. Most postings require learning skills.

Socioemotional skills. Most postings require responsability, decency, perseverance, accuracy, attentiveness, and hardworking.

Management

This professional area includes chief executives, directors, and department managers.

Education and experience. Three-quarters of postings—more than any other professional area—included education requirements (in business administration, economics, marketing, finance, engineering, or law) and required complete higher education. Virtually all postings required job experience; more than 28 percent required at least five years of experience (the highest percentage of any professional area).

Technical skills. Most postings required knowledge of specific region, market, industry, and technologies; legislation (corporate, civil, commercial, labor, administrative, tax, land, and procedural law); personnel and crisis management; strategic planning and budgeting; and marketing and sales skills.

Computer skills. Most postings did not cite special requirements (probably because such skills are taken for granted). About a quarter of postings required knowledge of basic computer tools (Word, Excel, and Internet).

Foreign language. About 30 percent of postings required knowledge of English, sometimes together with another language (Russian, Spanish, Portuguese, Danish, Vietnamese, or Arabic).

Cognitive skills. Most postings required communication, management, thinking (analytical and strategic thinking), decision-making, and problem-solving skills.

Socioemotional skills. Most postings required goal orientation, negotiation, responsibility, stress management, leadership, organization, self-management.

Other. Some postings required willingness to travel and work overtime; charisma.

Manufacturing

This professional area includes several occupational groups, from machine tool operators to chief engineers and directors. Postings for managers, engineers (including occupational safety engineers), technologists, and engineering science technicians from higher-skilled occupation categories (ISCO classification groups 1–3) accounted for almost three-quarters of postings in the sample. The following job requirements therefore focus exclusively on this segment.

Education and experience. Most job postings cited education (mainly higher technical level, reported in about three-quarters of postings) and experience (at least two years in 60 percent of postings).

Technical skills. Most postings required the ability to prepare technological documentation and understand drawings, technologies; production processes and materials; regulations on certain products (such as medicines and food); and rules governing occupational safety, fire and industrial safety, and construction and installation works.

Computer skills. More than half of postings did not require computer skills. About one-third required basic computer tools (MS Office, Internet, e-mail, sometimes the accounting software 1C). Many required advanced computer skills and proficiency in special software for two- and three-dimensional modeling and design (such as Solidworks, KOMPAS, AutoCAD, and ESKD) or graphic design (such as Adobe Photoshop, Adobe Illustrator, and CorelDraw).

Foreign language. More than 85 percent of postings included foreign language requirements; most required technical English.

Cognitive skills. Most postings required communication and thinking skills.

Socioemotional skills. Most postings required responsibility, organization, leadership, proactiveness and initiative, perseverance, and attentiveness.

Marketing, Advertising, and Public Relations

This professional area includes mainly professionals in marketing and advertising (including account, brand, and product managers; market researchers; and regional representatives). It also includes art designers, copywriters, and administrators. The analysis excluded the large number of postings posted by Kobzov Circus, an entertainment firm. Before their exclusion, it had the largest number of postings not including any education (70 percent).

Education and experience. Job postings cited work experience and skills requirements more often than formal education. Only 40 percent of postings included educational requirements (mainly higher education, although some entry-level positions were open to students with incomplete education). By contrast, 70 percent required at least one year of experience.

Technical skills. Most postings required knowledge of specific markets, proficiency in marketing tools and brand development (often related to online marketing), data analysis, hand drawing, and visualization skills.

Computer skills. Most postings did not cite computer skills requirements. Those that did required basic tools (mainly Word, Excel, and Internet); knowledge of the standard package of graphics software for graphic designers (Adobe Illustrator, Adobe Photoshop, Adobe InDesign, and CorelDraw); and knowledge of statistics tools and Web Analytics systems (including Adriver, Google Analytics, Yandex Metrics, Gemius) for e-advertising specialists and market and business analysts.

Foreign language. One in three postings required fluency in a foreign language (mainly English, sometimes Russian).

Cognitive skills. Most postings required communication (oral and written, presentation), learning, time management, and thinking skills.

Socioemotional skills. Most postings required responsability, creativity, goal orientation, teamwork, attention to detail, and negotiation.

Medicine and Pharmaceuticals

This professional area includes representatives of pharmaceutical companies, pharmacists, medical doctors, and nurses.

Education and experience. Nearly three-quarters of postings required at least incomplete higher education, and almost 60 percent required completed higher education, mainly in pharmacy, medicine, chemistry, or biology. More than 90 percent of postings required at least one year of relevant work experience.

Technical skills. Knowledge of pharmacology and the pharmaceutical market, knowledge of marketing and experience in promoting drugs (for medical representatives and pharmacists), and knowledge and practice of auditing management systems (for specialists in certification and standardization).

Computer skills. More than half of postings required computers skills (particularly for medical and pharmaceutical representatives).

Foreign language. Twenty percent of postings required good command of English.

Cognitive skills. Most postings required communication and learning skills.

Socioemotional skills. Most postings required responsibility, goal orientation, professionalism, initiative, attentiveness, and agreeableness (politeness).

Other. Some postings required the willingness to travel (for medical representatives).

Sales

This professional area includes sales managers, heads of sales departments, and specialists in foreign trade activities.

Education and experience. Half of postings did not cite an educational requirement. The other half required higher education, most often in economics, management, marketing, or international economic relations; education in technical fields and agriculture was also listed. Three-fourths of postings required one to four years of experience. Many listings indicated that they give priority to candidates with their own base of customers and suppliers.

Technical skills. Most postings required knowledge of specific markets and products (competitors, prices, major suppliers, and technical characteristics of products); market analysis and pricing; and international commercial terms.

Computer skills. About half of postings required basic computer skills (mainly Word, Excel, Internet, and e-mail).

Foreign language. About 30 percent of postings required fluency in a foreign language (English in all cases, sometimes along with German, Spanish, French, Arabic, or Polish).

Cognitive skills. Most postings required communication (including presentation) and time management skills.

Socioemotional skills. Most postings required responsability, proactiveness, goal orientation, self-management, stress management, negotiation, teamwork, and cooperation.

Sports Clubs, Fitness Clubs, and Beauty Salons

This professional area includes administrators of sports facilities, fitness and sport instructors, and employees of beauty salons (cosmetologists, makeup artists, massage therapists, hairdressers, manicurists, and pedicurists).

Education and experience. Sixty-eight percent of postings did not include an educational requirement. Postings that did usually required only specialized secondary education (incomplete higher) or specialized training courses. Eighty percent of postings required at least a year of relevant work experience.

Technical skills. Requirements varied. Employees are often responsible for finding new clients, providing information about services of the company, working with databases of clients, and scheduling.

Computer and foreign language skills. Only 10 percent of postings included requirements regarding computer skills or English.

Cognitive skills. Most postings required communication, learning, and time management skills.

Socioemotional skills. Most postings responsibility, orderliness, professionalism, and agreeableness.

Tourism, Hotels, and Restaurants

This professional area includes travel agents (including ticket sellers); cooks; and administrators and managers of restaurants, bars, and hotels.

Education and experience. Relevant experience is required more often (82 percent of postings) than education (32 percent).

Technical skills. Depends on occupation; many postings include none.

Computer skills. No special requirements in most cases. A quarter of postings required knowledge of basic computer tools.

Foreign language. A quarter of postings indicated that knowledge of English is preferred.

Cognitive skills. Most vacancies required communication skills.

Socioemotional skills. Most vacancies required agreeableness and hospitality for travel agents; responsibility, stress management, goal orientation, being hardworking, perseverance, orderliness, and creativity (for cooks).

Transport and Logistics

This professional area includes logistics managers (specialists) and drivers, mainly taxi drivers, who are required to have a driver's license and often own a car.

Education and experience. Three-quarters of postings required relevant experience. About two-fifths required education (higher education).

Technical skills. For logistics managers, knowledge of the transport logistics market; basic principles of tenders and negotiations; knowledge of customs clearance procedures, international commercial terms, and customs legislation; and ability to fill out customs declarations.

Computer skills. Forty percent of postings required knowledge of basic computer tools (MS Word and Excel), with proficiency in the accounting software 1C.

Foreign language. About a quarter of postings (mainly for positions dealing with international transport services) required an advanced level of English.

Cognitive skills. Communication, thinking, and time management skills.

Socioemotional skills. Most postings required responsability, negotiation, stress management, goal orientation, agreeableness (politeness), and professionalism.

Other. Some postings required willingness to work long, irregular hours and travel; neat appearance.

Environmental Benefits Statement

The World Bank Group is committed to reducing its environmental footprint. In support of this commitment, we leverage electronic publishing options and print-on-demand technology, which is located in regional hubs worldwide. Together, these initiatives enable print runs to be lowered and shipping distances decreased, resulting in reduced paper consumption, chemical use, greenhouse gas emissions, and waste.

We follow the recommended standards for paper use set by the Green Press Initiative. The majority of our books are printed on Forest Stewardship Council (FSC)–certified paper, with nearly all containing 50–100 percent recycled content. The recycled fiber in our book paper is either unbleached or bleached using totally chlorine-free (TCF), processed chlorine–free (PCF), or enhanced elemental chlorine–free (EECF) processes.

More information about the Bank's environmental philosophy can be found at http://www.worldbank.org/corporateresponsibility.